Standard Grade | General | Credit

History

General Level 2005

Credit Level 2005

General Level 2006

Credit Level 2006

General Level 2007

Credit Level 2007

Leckie × Leckie

First exam published in 2005.
Published by Leckie & Leckie Ltd, 3rd Floor, 4 Queen Street, Edinburgh EH2 1JE
tel: 0131 220 6831 fax: 0131 225 9987 enquiries@leckieandleckie.co.uk www.leckieandleckie.co.uk

ISBN 978-1-84372-515-2

A CIP Catalogue record for this book is available from the British Library.

Printed in Scotland by Scotprint.

Leckie & Leckie is a division of Huveaux plc.

Leckie & Leckie is grateful to the copyright holders, as credited at the back of the book, for permission to use their material.
Every effort has been made to trace the copyright holders and to obtain their permission for the use of copyright material.
Leckie & Leckie will gladly receive information enabling them to rectify any error or omission in subsequent editions.

[BLANK PAGE]

G

1540/402

<table>
<tr><td>NATIONAL
QUALIFICATIONS
2005</td><td>MONDAY, 16 MAY
10.20 AM – 11.50 AM</td><td>HISTORY
STANDARD GRADE
General Level</td></tr>
</table>

Answer questions from Unit I **and** Unit II **and** Unit III.

Choose only **one** Context from each Unit and answer Sections A **and** B. The Contexts chosen should be those you have studied.

The Contexts in each Unit are:

You must use the information in the sources, and your own knowledge, to answer the questions.

Number the questions as shown in the question paper.

Some sources have been adapted or translated.

SCOTTISH
QUALIFICATIONS
AUTHORITY

©

UNIT I—CHANGING LIFE IN SCOTLAND AND BRITAIN

CONTEXT A: 1750s–1850s

SECTION A: KNOWLEDGE AND UNDERSTANDING

Study the information in the sources. You must also use your own knowledge in your answers.

Source A is from the Old Statistical Account for Gargunnock in Stirlingshire, written in 1797.

Source A

> Great improvement is being made in the art of ploughing. Prizes are given annually by the wealthy land owners in the area to those who plough best and the tenant farmers eagerly compete for this honour. The Old Scots Plough is most generally used but Small's new plough is beginning to be preferred. A threshing machine has been set up by some farmers. It is one of the most useful farming machines ever invented.

1. How important was new technology in Scottish farms in the late eighteenth century? 4

Source B describes housing in the Scottish countryside.

Source B

> The form of dwelling most often seen was the longhouse or byre-dwelling. This, in its later eighteenth-century form, consisted of a drystone-built structure with an interior divided into living quarters and space for cattle. The floor was usually of stamped earth with the fireplace in the centre of the floor.

2. Describe housing in the Scottish countryside in the eighteenth century. 3

Marks

SECTION B: ENQUIRY SKILLS

The issue for investigating is:

> Moving from the countryside to the town was good for all Scots in the period 1750–1850.

Study the sources carefully and answer the questions which follow.

You should use your own knowledge where appropriate.

Source C was written in the early nineteenth century by Gilbert Burns, brother of Robert Burns, the famous poet.

Source C

> I often heard our father describe the sadness he felt when he had to leave *his* father's farm and move away. He and his brother parted on top of a hill overlooking their beloved countryside, each going off in search of employment. Our father first moved to Edinburgh where he found employment. There was no work on the farm and those were difficult times for farmers. Farming was an uncertain business then and many were forced to move away from the countryside.

3. How useful is **Source C** for investigating population movement in Scotland between 1750 and 1850?   **3**

Source D is from "The Scottish Nation" by T. M. Devine.

Source D

> In 1750 only one tenth of the Scottish population lived in towns. By 1850 more Scots lived in towns than in almost any other country in Europe. Newspapers were remarking on the number of workers leaving the countryside or coming down from the Highlands, driven as much by misery at home as by new opportunities and employment in the Lowland towns. Scottish factory owners needed to attract such migrants and population movement was a bonus for manufacturers keen to hire more labour.

4. What evidence is there in **Source C** that moving from the countryside to the town was **not** good for Scottish people?

   What evidence is there in **Source D** that moving from the countryside to the town was good for Scottish people?   **5**

5. How far do you agree that moving from the countryside to the town was good for all Scots in the period 1750–1850?   **4**

   You must use evidence **from the sources** and **your own knowledge** to come to a conclusion.

[END OF CONTEXT IA]

Now turn to the Context you have studied in Unit II

Marks

UNIT I—CHANGING LIFE IN SCOTLAND AND BRITAIN

CONTEXT B: 1830s–1930s

SECTION A: KNOWLEDGE AND UNDERSTANDING

Study the information in the sources. You must also use your own knowledge in your answers.

Source A is about the effects of new technology on the early days of railways.

Source A

> The idea of railway tracks was not new. Wagonways with wooden rails had been used to make it easier to move horse-drawn trucks carrying coal. Several inventions helped to create the Railway Age and, by 1832, steam locomotives were in regular use enabling trains to travel at over 30 miles an hour. Greater speeds were also made possible by the development of heavier steel rails and improvements in signalling made travelling safer.

1. How important was new technology in the development of railways?   **4**

Source B describes housing in an area of the Scottish countryside in the nineneenth century.

Source B

> It was quite unusual for farm workers to settle in a farm for much more than two or three years. They lived in tied cottages provided as part of the deal on pay. Most farm workers' dwellings were single roomed. The walls were less than two metres high. There was no ceiling as such. The room was divided inside by wooden box beds.

2. Describe housing in the Scottish countryside in the nineteenth century.   **3**

SECTION B: ENQUIRY SKILLS

The issue for investigating is:

> The arrival of Irish immigrants brought benefits for all Scots.

Study the sources carefully and answer the questions which follow.

You should use your own knowledge where appropriate.

Source C is evidence given to a Parliamentary Enquiry in 1836 by Alexander Carlisle who ran a spinning mill in Paisley.

Source C

> Our mills never would have grown so rapidly if we had not had large numbers of Irish families. The work of this town requires women and children as well as men. Without the Irish, a sufficient number of workers would never have been found. The large immigration of the Irish at the harvest season also proves a great advantage to our farmers.

3. How useful is **Source C** for investigating the results of Irish immigration into Scotland?

3

Source D is from "Changing Life in Scotland and Britain".

Source D

> Many native Scots resented the Irish. They accused them of dragging down wages. While this was undoubtedly true, it has to be counterbalanced by saying that by 1880 they were becoming prominent in Trade Unions and were helping to push up wages. However, the arrival of large numbers of desperately poor Irish did nothing to ease the already overcrowded housing situation. Moreover, their arrival sometimes increased existing tensions over religious beliefs and practices.

4. What evidence is there in **Source C** that the arrival of Irish immigrants brought benefits?

   What evidence is there in **Source D** that the arrival of Irish immigrants did **not** bring benefits?

5

5. How far do you agree that the arrival of Irish immigrants brought benefits for all Scots?

4

   You must use evidence **from the sources** and **your own knowledge** to come to a conclusion.

[END OF CONTEXT IB]

Now turn to the Context you have studied in Unit II

UNIT I—CHANGING LIFE IN SCOTLAND AND BRITAIN

CONTEXT C: 1880s–Present Day

SECTION A: KNOWLEDGE AND UNDERSTANDING

Study the information in the sources. You must also use your own knowledge in your answers.

Source A is from "Change in Scotland, 1830–1930" by W. Doran and R. Dargie, published in 1994.

Source A

> The Equal Pay Act said men and women should be paid the same wage for doing the same work. Between 1970 and 1975 women's earnings rose from 63% to 72% of men's wages. They have remained about the same ever since. Some employers got round this by transferring women to jobs where there are no male workers to compare themselves with.

1. How important was the introduction of new laws in improving employment and working conditions for women?　　　　**4**

In **Source B** Jean Whittle describes living in a house in the countryside near Jedburgh in the 1920s.

Source B

> We lived in one part of a house, with my father's parents. There was always an apprentice lived with us. Quite often there would be fifteen of us in the building. I well remember how the grown-ups were served their meals first. The water had to be carried into the house from a tap a few yards away. There was a separate building called the "wash house" where the scrubbing of clothes was done.

2. Describe housing in the countryside in early twentieth-century Scotland.　　　　**3**

Marks

SECTION B: ENQUIRY SKILLS

The issue for investigating is:

> The arrival of immigrants was good for Scotland.

Study the sources carefully and answer the questions which follow.

You should use your own knowledge where appropriate.

In **Source C** Mary McEwan writes about the 1930s in "I Can Remember", published in 1976.

Source C

> The Italians in Glasgow were always friendly. I liked their cafes which stayed open a' the time and sold fags, ice cream and fish and chips. I loved to sit in them wi' ma friends and listen to the waiters chattering in Italian and many girls went out with them later. It brought a new dimension to the drab city. It was somewhere warm and cheerful away frae ma single end (house).

3. How useful is **Source C** for investigating the impact of immigrants on Scotland? **3**

Source D is from "The Scottish Nation" by T.M. Devine.

Source D

> A Parliamentary Committee suggested that Italian ice-cream parlours were lowering moral standards as the owners allowed young people of both sexes to meet there after proper opening hours and sometimes misbehave themselves. After closing time, at 10.00 pm on a Saturday in Glasgow, many went to buy their fish suppers. The food was not always consumed peacefully and the police had to be called to control fights. However, all in all, the Italians attracted much less hostility than did the Irish and the Lithuanians.

4. What evidence in **Source C** agrees with the view that the arrival of immigrants was good for Scotland?

   What evidence in **Source D** disagrees with the view that the arrival of immigrants was good for Scotland? **5**

5. How far do you agree that the arrival of immigrants was good for Scotland? **4**

   You must use evidence **from the sources** and **your own knowledge** to come to a conclusion.

[END OF CONTEXT IC]

Now turn to the Context you have studied in Unit II

Marks

UNIT II—INTERNATIONAL COOPERATION AND CONFLICT

CONTEXT A: 1790s–1820s

SECTION A: KNOWLEDGE AND UNDERSTANDING

Study the information in the sources. You must also use your own knowledge in your answers.

Source A is from "The Fourth Coalition" by Peter Lane.

Source A

> There was a brief break in the years of warfare during most of 1813. Napoleon used this opportunity to build up a new army, but it now contained many poorly trained men. Meanwhile, the Austrians, Prussians and Russians joined Britain in the Fourth Coalition. The Allied armies closed in on Napoleon's troops who were then defeated at the Battle of the Nations in October.

1. Explain why the Fourth Coalition was able to defeat Napoleon.

3

Source B is from the National Maritime Museum's website.

Source B

> Punishments at sea were designed as warnings to others. Of course, some captains were more cruel than others but even Admiral Nelson, who cared for his men, found it necessary to condemn sailors to harsh floggings. Seamen could also be "tarred and feathered" or tied to a rope, swung overboard and dragged round the underneath of the ship.

2. How important was harsh punishment as a cause of complaint on board ships in Nelson's navy?

4

Marks

SECTION B: ENQUIRY SKILLS

The following sources are about the Congress of Vienna.

Study the sources carefully and answer the questions which follow.

You should use your own knowledge where appropriate.

Source C was written by Lewis Goldsmith in 1822.

Source C

> The monarchs and important ministers at the Congress of Vienna were almost wholly occupied by promoting their own power and strength. They neglected to take measures for preserving future peace. They showed the most unfortunate ignorance of public feeling. They should have known that people do not like being moved from ruler to ruler.

3. What did Lewis Goldsmith think about the Congress of Vienna? **3**

Source D is about the Congress of Vienna and is from "www.napoleonguide.com".

Source D

> The powerful delegates at Vienna decided not to punish France too severely. While a workable peace was the main aim, the delegates also wanted to restore the legitimate rulers of Europe and to increase their power. Prussia and Russia wanted to divide up Saxony and this annoyed Austria. Poland was now ruled by the Russian tsar and many Poles were unhappy.

4. To what extent do **Sources C** and **D** agree about the Congress of Vienna? **4**

[END OF CONTEXT IIA]

Now turn to the Context you have studied in Unit III

Marks

UNIT II—INTERNATIONAL COOPERATION AND CONFLICT

CONTEXT B: 1890s–1920s

SECTION A: KNOWLEDGE AND UNDERSTANDING

Study the information in the sources. You must also use your own knowledge in your answers.

Source A is from "The First World War" by John Keegan.

Source A

> Almost one month after they had been blamed for the assassinations at Sarajevo, the Serbian government received the ultimatum from Austria-Hungary. At first, they thought they would have to give in and accept all ten points. However, on hearing that Russia was very much on their side, they decided to attach conditions to six points and to reject absolutely the most important point. On hearing this, Austria-Hungary declared war on Serbia.

  1. Explain why Austria-Hungary went to war against Serbia in 1914.   **3**

Source B is from "Landships" by David Fletcher.

Source B

> The British tanks, in three great waves, rolled down on the German defences at Cambrai. Working to a pre-arranged pattern, the tanks easily crossed the main trench lines and pushed on, with the German infantry scattering before them. However, if the success came as a surprise to the Germans, the British Command were also surprised as they had not expected such a breakthrough and had no reserves to exploit it.

  2. How important was the tank as a weapon in the First World War?   **4**

Marks

SECTION B: ENQUIRY SKILLS

The following sources are about the Treaty of Versailles.

Study the sources carefully and answer the questions which follow.

You should use your own knowledge where appropriate.

Source C was written by British Prime Minister, David Lloyd George, about the Treaty of Versailles.

Source C

> I cannot imagine any greater cause of war than surrounding the German people with a number of small states containing large masses of Germans demanding reunion with their native land. The Treaty will strip Germany of her colonies and reduce her army to a mere police force. If Germany feels she has been unjustly treated she will seek revenge.

3. What did Lloyd George think about the Treaty of Versailles? 　　3

Source D is from "Mein Kampf" by Adolf Hitler.

Source D

> In the year 1919, the German people were burdened with the unjust peace treaty. You would have thought that the cry for German freedom would have been loudly promoted by the government but it was not. The Treaty was a shame and a disgrace. It must be our aim to get back to Germany the land and the people to which we are entitled. State boundaries are made by man and can be changed by man and *we will* change them when our army is restored to its full strength.

4. How far do **Sources C** and **D** agree about the Treaty of Versailles? 　　4

[END OF CONTEXT IIB]

Now turn to the Context you have studied in Unit III

Marks

UNIT II—INTERNATIONAL COOPERATION AND CONFLICT

CONTEXT C: 1930s–1960s

SECTION A: KNOWLEDGE AND UNDERSTANDING

Study the information in the sources. You must also use your own knowledge in your answers.

Source A describes the effects of German rearmament.

Source A

> In 1934 Hitler gave top secret orders for the armed forces to expand. This was forbidden by the Treaty of Versailles. In 1935 Hitler cast off the cloak of secrecy and announced that there would be compulsory military service. The countries around Germany were alarmed and quickly began making alliances with each other in case Germany attacked one of them.

1. Explain why German rearmament led to increased tension in Europe.

3

Source B describes when the Atom bomb was dropped on Hiroshima on 6th August 1945.

Source B

> The bomb fell for 53 seconds and exploded at about 1800 feet above the ground. What followed was the greatest man-made explosion ever seen at that time. More than 60,000 buildings were destroyed as a huge fire storm raged across the city. Possibly 80,000 were killed and thousands were injured as a giant mushroom cloud rose over the city.

2. How important was the use of the Atom bomb in the conduct of the war against Japan?

4

Marks

SECTION B: ENQUIRY SKILLS

The following sources are about the Cuban Missile Crisis.

Study the sources carefully and answer the questions which follow.

You should use your own knowledge where appropriate.

Source C was written by the Russian leader, Khrushchev, in his memoirs.

Source C

> One thought kept hammering away at my brain: "What will happen if we lose Cuba?" If Cuba fell, other Latin American countries would reject us. I had to answer the American threat but still avoid war. I had the idea of putting missiles on Cuba without letting the United States know. Our missiles would, I thought, stop America from taking action against Cuba's government. As well as protecting Cuba, the Americans would also learn what it feels like to have enemy missiles pointing at you.

3. What was Khrushchev's opinion on the placing of missiles on Cuba?   3

Source D is an American view of the Cuban Missile Crisis.

Source D

> The defence of Cuba did not really need the introduction of long-range nuclear missiles. One can be sure that Khrushchev took the decision to place missiles on Cuba, not for Cuban reasons but for Russian reasons. He would have placed 64 Soviet missiles—all effective against America. Every country in the world watching such a cheeky action, just ninety miles from the United States, would wonder whether it would ever again trust America's resolve.

4. To what extent do **Sources C** and **D** agree about why missiles were placed on Cuba?   4

[END OF CONTEXT IIC]

Now turn to the Context you have studied in Unit III

Marks

UNIT III—PEOPLE AND POWER

CONTEXT A: USA 1850–1880

SECTION A: KNOWLEDGE AND UNDERSTANDING

Study the information in the sources. You must also use your own knowledge in your answers.

Source A is about Abraham Lincoln and the Union.

Source A

> When Abraham Lincoln became President in March 1861, Fort Sumter was still under Government control. Southerners had been talking about secession for many years. Lincoln's duty as President of the United States was to protect the Constitution. Lincoln said that he must hold **all** the property belonging to the Government. He also said that he must collect **all** the taxes due to the Government.

1. Explain why Abraham Lincoln wanted to preserve the Union. 3

Source B describes the work of the Freedmen's Bureau.

Source B

> The Freedmen's Bureau had been established in 1865, while the war was still going on. It was used to supply food to ex-slaves. It also provided hospitals. The Freedmen's Bureau also supervised ex-slaves' contracts with plantation owners. It offered to rent them land that had been taken from the Confederates.

2. Describe the work of the Freedmen's Bureau after the Civil War. 3

Marks

SECTION B: ENQUIRY SKILLS

The following sources are about slavery in the South before the Civil War.

Study the sources carefully and answer the questions which follow.

You should use your own knowledge where appropriate.

Source C is a drawing which appeared in a Southern magazine before the Civil War.

Source C

Happy slaves dance on their Southern Plantation.

3. How useful is **Source C** as evidence of the conditions of slaves before 1860?   **4**

Source D is taken from a book about Civil Rights.

Source D

> Slaves were regarded as property. The point of their existence was to work for their owners. Most were given little or no education. Families could be broken up, children could be sold without their parents. Housing was often of the poorest and most basic. Many slaves were cruelly treated and lived in great unhappiness.

4. How far do **Sources C** and **D** disagree about the treatment of slaves in the South?   **3**

Source E is about slave resistance.

Source E

> Slaves did not always accept the way they were treated without protest. Slaves often tried to run away. About 1,000 slaves a year escaped. From time to time slave rebellions occurred. The possibility of such revolts terrified the South. Usually, however, protest took simpler forms. Some slaves pretended to be ill to stop them from working. Other common ways of protest were deliberately misunderstanding instructions or working slowly.

5. How fully does **Source E** describe the actions taken by slaves against their slavery?   **4**

    You must use evidence **from the sources** and **from your own knowledge** and give reasons for your answer.

[END OF CONTEXT IIIA]

Marks

UNIT III— PEOPLE AND POWER

CONTEXT B: INDIA 1917–1947

SECTION A: KNOWLEDGE AND UNDERSTANDING

Study the information in the sources. You must also use your own knowledge in your answers.

Source A is from the memoirs of a British missionary in India.

Source A

> I went to India at the age of thirty-three. Before then I never heard one single word of blame with regard to British rule in India. The idea was always impressed on me that British management of the Indian continent was the most glorious event in the whole of British History. British rule in India was indeed something I agreed with.

1. Explain why many British people agreed with British rule in India.　　　3

Source B is from a British military newspaper in 1919.

Source B

> India has just come out of the Great War. In the events recently seen at Amritsar, General Dyer had only his Indian troops and police to keep order. Dyer's men had toured the city for two hours. There was then an attempt by some Indians to hold a banned public meeting. As the crowd refused to disperse, the order to fire was given. There were heavy casualties amongst the mob.

2. Describe the events at Amritsar in April 1919.　　　3

Marks

SECTION B: ENQUIRY SKILLS

The following sources are about India before Independence.

Read the sources carefully and answer the questions which follow.

You should use your own knowledge where appropriate.

Source C is a David Low cartoon from the London Evening Standard in 1928.

Source C

UNITED INDIA.
The peoples of India are united in their opposition to British rule.

3. How useful is **Source C** as evidence of the desire for Indian Independence?   **4**

Source D is from "Divide and Quit" by Penderel Moon.

Source D

> The Congress Party was important to many Indians who longed for an end to British rule. Such an organisation, headed and symbolised by Gandhi, had emotional and religious appeal to the Hindu peoples but it did not always appeal to the Muslims. Gandhi often claimed that he brought all groups together: that he was "a Muslim, a Hindu, a Buddhist and a Parsee". This claim, however, was not believed by all the different religious groups in India.

4. How far do **Sources C** and **D** agree about how united the people of India were in their desire for an independent India?   **3**

Source E is by a modern Indian historian.

Source E

> India was within reach of its Independence. The events of the Direct Action Day shocked and split many Indian people. The Congress Party had now formed a temporary Government. Mohammed Jinnah, the leader of the Muslim League, had decided to stay away. However he nominated five of his followers to join it, with orders to wreck it from within.

5. How fully does **Source E** explain the political differences inside India before Independence?   **4**

   You must use evidence **from the sources** and **from your own knowledge** and give reasons for your answer.

[END OF CONTEXT IIIB]

Marks

UNIT III—PEOPLE AND POWER

CONTEXT C: RUSSIA 1914–1941

SECTION A: KNOWLEDGE AND UNDERSTANDING

Study the information in the sources. You must also use your own knowledge in your answers.

Source A is from a secret Petrograd Police Report, dated October 1916.

Source A

> Military defeats have brought the people to a clearer understanding of war. It means unfair distribution of foodstuffs as well as an immense increase in the cost of living. Everywhere there are exceptional feelings of hostility and opposition to the government because of the unbearable burden of war and the worsening conditions of everyday life.

1. Explain why World War One caused growing discontent in Russia.   **3**

Source B is about the October Revolution in Russia.

Source B

> By 24th October the Red Guards were well armed and ready for action. During the night they began to take control of the most important locations in Petrograd. First, they took control of the six bridges across the River Neva. Then, in the morning, they seized the power station and the railway station. The Provisional Government had its headquarters in the Winter Palace and was guarded only by army cadets and the Women's Battalion.

2. Describe the main events of the Bolshevik seizure of power in October 1917.   **3**

Marks

SECTION B: ENQUIRY SKILLS

The following sources are about the Russian Civil War.

Study the sources carefully and answer the questions which follow.

You should use your own knowledge where appropriate.

Source C is a Bolshevik Civil War poster from 1919.

Source C

Denikin   Kolchak   Yudenich

Britain, France and the USA control the White commanders.

3. How useful is **Source C** as evidence of Russian attitudes towards the Whites during the Civil War?

4

Source D describes the Allied intervention in the Civil War.

Source D

> Britain, France and the USA, along with several other powers, sent help to the Whites. Allied intervention was half-hearted and ineffective and did little to help the White leaders, Kolchak, Denikin and Yudenich. The intervention of foreign countries in fact helped the Communists. They portrayed the Whites as being controlled by foreign powers, while they themselves were defenders of ordinary Russians from foreign invaders.

4. How far do **Sources C** and **D** agree about the Civil War?

3

In **Source E** a Red Army soldier describes the effects of Trotsky's leadership.

Source E

> The city of Gomel was about to fall into enemy hands when Trotsky arrived. Then everything changed and the tide turned. Trotsky's arrival meant that the city would not be abandoned. Trotsky paid a visit to the troops in the front lines where he made a speech. We were lifted by the energy he displayed and indeed by his very appearance wherever a critical situation arose.

5. How fully does **Source E** describe Trotsky's role in the Red Army's victory?

4

You must use evidence **from the sources** and **from your own knowledge** and give reasons for your answer.

[END OF CONTEXT IIIC]

Marks

UNIT III—PEOPLE AND POWER

CONTEXT D: GERMANY 1918–1939

SECTION A: KNOWLEDGE AND UNDERSTANDING

Study the information in the sources. You must also use your own knowledge in your answers.

In **Source A** a German soldier describes his return to Frankfurt in 1918.

Source A

> In October I had permission to go home. I was very much looking forward to this leave after the terrific battles we had been through. As I went through the streets of Frankfurt I was not saluted, even though I was an officer. There was hardly anything to buy and what there was, was rationed. I hadn't realised at the front just how fed up with the war people were.

1. Explain why, by late 1918, German civilians wanted the war to end.   **3**

Source B is about the Munich Putsch.

Source B

> During a time of political and economic chaos in Germany, Hitler decided to lead an uprising. On November 8th, 1923, Herr von Kahr, head of the Bavarian government, spoke at a big meeting in a beer cellar in Munich. With some Nazi supporters, Hitler went into the meeting. He waited until 600 SA men had surrounded the building and then 25 Nazis burst into the hall. Hitler declared that a national revolution had begun.

2. Describe the main events of the Munich Putsch in November 1923.   **3**

Marks

SECTION B: ENQUIRY SKILLS

The following sources are about the methods used by the Nazis to come to power.

Study the sources carefully and answer the questions which follow.

You should use your own knowledge where appropriate.

Source C is a Nazi poster from the early 1930s.

Source C

The SA march toward Aryan purity

3. How useful is **Source C** as evidence of what people in Germany thought of the SA in the 1930s?

4

Source D is from "Hitler and Germany" by B. J. Elliot.

Source D

> Some saw in the SA an appeal to their Aryan manhood. Some were attracted by the uniforms and badges, particularly the ex-soldiers. Some were impressed by the strength portrayed by the Brownshirts. Others who were repelled by Nazism, were, quite naturally, frightened into silence. Hitler believed that the SA was his trump card and went out of his way to glorify as heroes those members who were killed or wounded.

4. To what extent do **Sources C** and **D** agree on the ways the SA was made to appeal to Germans?

3

Source E was written by an American who had attended a Nazi rally.

Source E

> The hall was a sea of brightly coloured flags. Hitler's arrival was dramatic. The band stopped playing. There was a hush over the 30,000 people packed into the hall. Hitler appeared and strode slowly down the centre aisle while 30,000 hands were raised in salute. In such an atmosphere no wonder that every word spoken by Hitler was greeted with enormous cheering.

5. How fully does **Source E** describe the appeal of Hitler to the German people in the 1930s?

4

You must use evidence **from the sources** and **from your own knowledge** and give reasons for your answer.

[END OF CONTEXT IIID]

[END OF QUESTION PAPER]

[BLANK PAGE]

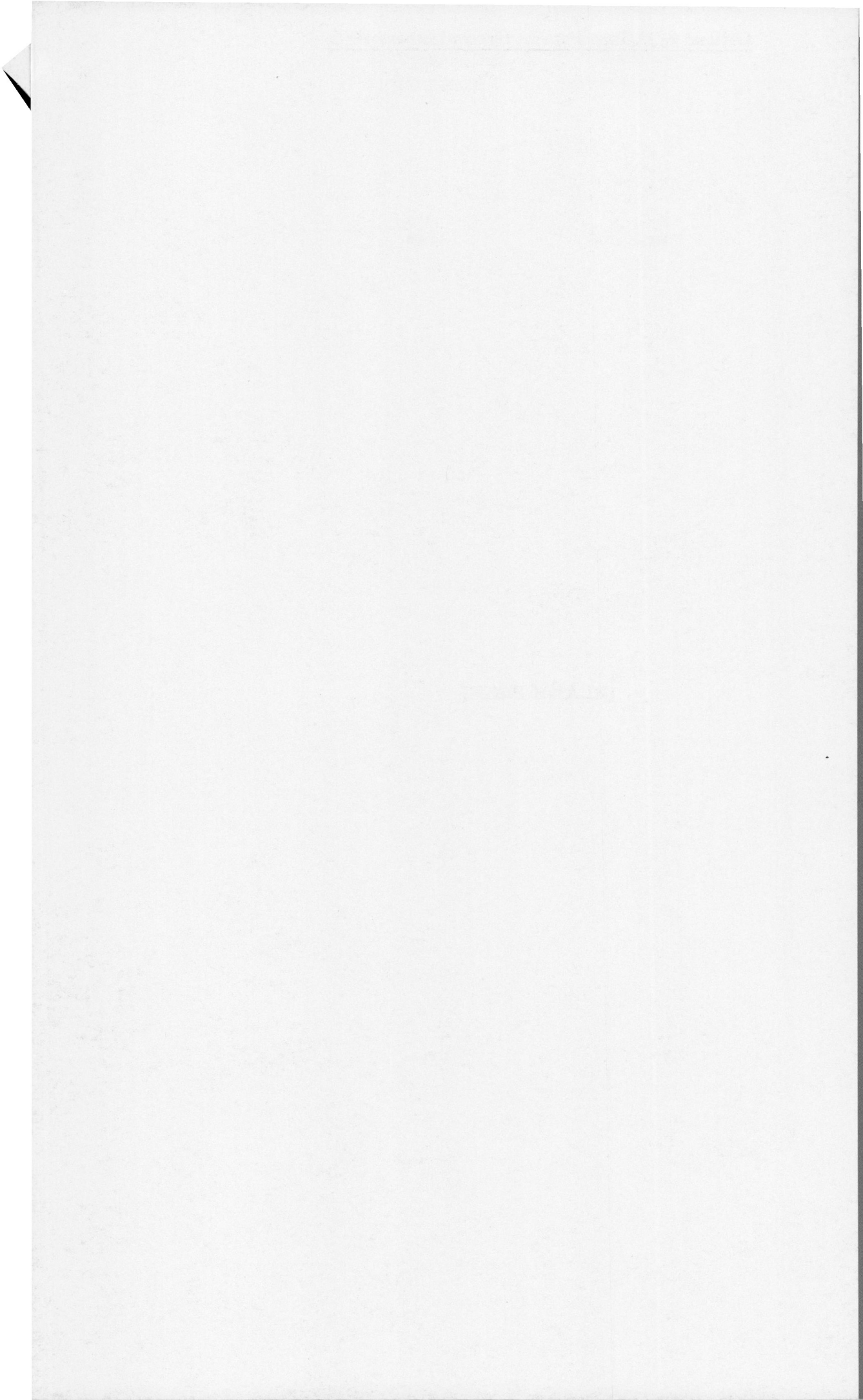

[BLANK PAGE]

C

1540/403

NATIONAL
QUALIFICATIONS
2005

MONDAY, 16 MAY
1.00 PM – 2.45 PM

HISTORY
STANDARD GRADE
Credit Level

Answer questions from Unit I **and** Unit II **and** Unit III.

Choose only **one** Context from each Unit and answer Sections A **and** B. The Contexts chosen should be those you have studied.

The Contexts in each Unit are:

Number the questions as shown in the question paper.

Some sources have been adapted or translated.

SCOTTISH
QUALIFICATIONS
AUTHORITY

Marks

UNIT I—CHANGING LIFE IN SCOTLAND AND BRITAIN

CONTEXT A: 1750s–1850s

SECTION A: KNOWLEDGE AND UNDERSTANDING

> In the first half of the nineteenth century, towns and cities were steadily becoming more lethal.

1. How far do you agree that cholera was the most important public health problem in Britain between 1800 and the 1850s?

5

> The Scottish electoral system in 1830 was totally unfair.

2. Describe some ways in which the 1832 Reform Act made Scotland more democratic.

3

SECTION B: ENQUIRY SKILLS

The issue for investigating is:

> Changes in textile manufacture brought major benefits for people in Scotland in the period 1750–1850.

Study the sources carefully and answer the questions which follow.
You should use your own knowledge where appropriate.

Source A was written by cotton manufacturer James Ogden in his "Description of Textile Manufacture" published in 1783.

Source A

> There is a huge demand for exports of textiles for foreign trade. There is also a growing demand for domestic use. No amount of effort by any number of workmen could have answered those demands without the introduction of the spinning machines. People saw how children, from nine to twelve years of age, could manage the machines easily and also bring plenty of money into families that before were poverty stricken and overburdened with children. Consequently, even more new machinery has been brought into the mills.

3. How useful is **Source A** for investigating textile manufacture in Scotland in the period 1750–1850?

4

Marks

Source B was written in "Scotland, A New History" by Professor of History, Michael Lynch, in 1992.

Source B

> The coming of cotton brought new-style discipline in the alien world of the factory for the spinners of yarn. It was an easily learned skill but practised in a hostile environment where heat and dust often caused tuberculosis. It was a trade for the young: almost two out of every three of both the male and female workforce were under twenty-one. The factory employed cheap labour from wherever it could get it. Cotton thread production brought with it an increased demand for handloom weavers.

Source C is from "Modern Scottish History" by A. Cooke and I. Donnachie, published in 1988.

Source C

> Although its aim was still to produce a more efficient and obedient workforce, Robert Owen's regime at New Lanark was better than elsewhere. There can be little doubt that, however unappealing factory work was at New Lanark, it was altogether more disagreeable elsewhere, especially in the smaller country mills and the urban factories of Glasgow and Paisley. The cotton-spinning industry grew so rapidly that by 1795 there were no fewer than ninety-one mills in Scotland.

Look at Sources A, B and C.

4. What evidence is there in the sources to support the view that changes in textile manufacture brought benefits for people in Scotland?

    What evidence in the sources **disagrees** with the view that changes in textile manufacture brought benefits for people in Scotland?　　　　　　　　　　　6

5. How far do you agree that changes in textile manufacture brought major benefits for people in Scotland in the period 1750–1850?

    You must use **evidence from the sources** and **your own knowledge** to reach a **balanced conclusion**.　　　　　　　　　　　5

[END OF CONTEXT IA]

Marks

UNIT I—CHANGING LIFE IN SCOTLAND AND BRITAIN

CONTEXT B: 1830s–1930s

SECTION A: KNOWLEDGE AND UNDERSTANDING

Worsening living conditions in the towns had a profound effect upon the public.

1. How far do you agree that cholera was the biggest health problem in nineteenth-century Britain?   **5**

Parliamentary reform in the early twentieth century marked another important step on the road to democracy.

2. Describe the ways in which the 1918 Reform Act made Britain more democratic.   **3**

SECTION B: ENQUIRY SKILLS

The issue for investigating is:

The coalmining industry brought benefits for people in Scotland in the nineteenth century.

Study the sources carefully and answer the questions which follow.
You should use your own knowledge where appropriate.

Source A is a description of the life of mine workers in Alloa, written by Robert Bald, a mining engineer in the first half of the nineteenth century.

Source A

The collier leaves his house for the pit along with his sons about eleven o' clock at night. About three hours after, his wife sets out for the pit having wrapped her infant in a blanket and left it to the care of an old woman who keeps three or four children at a time and feeds them with ale or whisky mixed with water. The mother descends the pit with her older daughters. It is no uncommon thing to see them, when coming back up again, weeping most bitterly from the excessive severity of the labour. But the instant they have laid down their burden, they resume their cheerfulness and return down the pit singing.

3. How useful is **Source A** for investigating coalmining in Scotland in the nineteenth century?   **4**

Marks

Source B is from "Changing Life in Scotland and Britain" by historians Ronald Cameron, Christine Henderson and Charles Robertson. It was published in the year 2000.

Source B

> During the nineteenth century there was a phenomenal growth in the coalmining industry due to increased demand for coal. Technological advances made it possible for more coal to be produced. New and deeper pits were developed. The production of coal became Scotland's largest industry, employing most workers. Whole new towns grew up around coalmining areas. Unfortunately, these were often places of dreadful overcrowding.

Source C is from "Years of Change" by J. Patrick and M. Packham, published in 1989.

Source C

> Miners could earn high wages. Mineowners expected them to work six days a week, but many worked only five. Even at that, their pay was nearly double that of many farm workers. But most miners lived in squalor. The women were expected to look after the home, but miners' wives also worked down the pit and had no energy to do housework. One doctor in Scotland noticed a fearful amount of filth accumulated on the walls and floors of miners' cottages.

Look at Sources A, B and C.

4. What evidence is there in the sources to support the view that coalmining brought benefits for people in Scotland?

   What evidence is there in the sources to suggest that coalmining did **not** bring benefits for people in Scotland? 6

5. How far do you agree that the coalmining industry brought benefits for people in Scotland in the nineteenth century?

   You must use **evidence from the sources** and **your own knowledge** to reach a **balanced conclusion**. 5

[END OF CONTEXT IB]

Marks

UNIT I—CHANGING LIFE IN SCOTLAND AND BRITAIN

CONTEXT C: 1880s–Present Day

SECTION A: KNOWLEDGE AND UNDERSTANDING

> By the early twentieth century, governments started to accept they had a role to play in improving the health of the population.

1. How far do you agree that government action was the most important factor in improving health in twentieth-century Britain?

5

> Parliamentary reform in the early twentieth century marked another important step on the road to democracy.

2. Describe the ways in which the 1918 Reform Act made Britain more democratic.

3

SECTION B: ENQUIRY SKILLS

The issue for investigating is:

> Changes in road transport brought benefits for people in Britain.

Study the sources carefully and answer the questions which follow. You should use your own knowledge where appropriate.

Source A is from the diary of Arthur Illingworth, written in the 1930s.

Source A

> By 1934 holidays were longer and I got paid during them. The motor car had brought adventure within everyone's reach, making accessible both highways and byways. On bank holidays the roadsides were littered with fathers of families mending tyres and crawling under vehicles, but this was part of the excitement of the new motoring craze. Families motored to lakes and to the seaside. Cobbled market squares filled up with traffic.

3. How useful is **Source A** for investigating the effects of road transport on the people of Britain?

4

Marks

Source B is an extract from "A Social and Economic History of Industrial Britain" by historian John Robottom, published in 1986.

Source B

> With every year, the number of motor vehicles increased rapidly. In addition, many towns were cut in two by roads which no one could cross safely. There was also the problem of rising health dangers from noise and fumes. One solution was to build motorways which helped traffic move faster and drew vehicles away from town bottlenecks. However, the new roads affected and often disturbed many lives. Houses were cleared to make way for them and people living near them had to use double glazing to cut down on the noise.

Source C is an extract from "A Century in Photographs – Travel" by Ian Harrison, published in 2000.

Source C

> Although Britain's motorways are now hopelessly overcrowded, they have certainly cut journey times. They have also reduced fatal accidents to less than half the level on ordinary roads, although two lorry drivers were killed in the M1's first fatal accident within a week of it opening. Motorways are notorious, too, for the damage they do to our landscape. They need an enormous amount of space and resources. Even in 1972 the cost of building a motorway was about £2 million per mile.

Look at Sources A, B and C.

4. What evidence is there in the sources that changes in road transport brought benefits for the people of Britain?

    What evidence is there in the sources that changes in road transport did **not** benefit the people of Britain?   6

5. How far do you agree that changes in road transport brought benefits for people in Britain in the twentieth century?

    You must use **evidence from the sources** and **your own knowledge** to reach a **balanced conclusion**.   5

[END OF CONTEXT IC]

Marks

UNIT II—INTERNATIONAL COOPERATION AND CONFLICT

CONTEXT A: 1790s–1820s

SECTION A: KNOWLEDGE AND UNDERSTANDING

> "The British Isles are declared to be in a state of blockade." Article 1 of the Berlin Decrees, 1806.

1. Explain why the French Wars affected the lives of British civilians.   **4**

> Castlereagh intended the Congresses to have very limited functions.

2. Describe the difficulties faced by the Congress System in keeping international peace between 1815 and 1825.   **4**

SECTION B: ENQUIRY SKILLS

The following sources are about the causes of the Revolutionary War.

**Study the sources carefully and answer the questions which follow.
You should use your own knowledge where appropriate.**

Source A is from a speech given by Prime Minister William Pitt to the House of Commons in February, 1793.

Source A

> The highly provocative French decrees of late 1792 promised military assistance to any European people wishing to depose its rulers. Now, the French nation is insisting upon the opening of the River Scheldt. We cannot stand by as indifferent spectators while France tramples upon the ancient treaties of our allies. We cannot view with indifference the progress of French ambition and of French arms. We must declare our resolution to oppose the ambitions of a nation which has murdered its monarch and which will destroy Britain, Europe and the World.

3. How useful is **Source A** as evidence of why Britain went to war with France in 1793?   **4**

Source B is from "Modern British History" by G.W. Southgate.

Source B

> The killing of Louis XVI destroyed any sympathy which many had felt for a people struggling for liberty. The Edict of Fraternity might have resulted in war but a French agent in London offered an explanation of the Edict which postponed the crisis. However, the opening of the River Scheldt to navigation, in defiance of international treaties, made a conflict unavoidable.

4. How far do **Sources A** and **B** agree about the causes of the French Revolutionary War?   **5**

[END OF CONTEXT IIA]

UNIT II—INTERNATIONAL COOPERATION AND CONFLICT

CONTEXT B: 1890s–1920s

SECTION A: KNOWLEDGE AND UNDERSTANDING

> Soldiers on the Western Front went through an enormous range of experiences.

1. Explain why the experiences of soldiers on the Western Front changed their attitudes towards the war.

    4

> "The work of the League of Nations will be fair and just, but it will need the support of the combined power of the great nations." President Woodrow Wilson, 1919.

2. Describe the difficulties faced by the League of Nations in keeping international peace between 1919 and 1928.

    4

SECTION B: ENQUIRY SKILLS

The following sources are about the causes of the First World War.

Study the sources carefully and answer the questions which follow.
You should use your own knowledge where appropriate.

Source A was written by Herbert Sulzbach in his diary on August 1st, 1914.

Source A

> Our Glorious Kaiser has ordered general mobilisation of the army and navy. Try as I might, I can't convey the splendid spirit and wild enthusiasm that has come over us all. We have always felt that Russia was going to attack us and now the idea that we are going to be able to defend ourselves gives us unbelievable strength. Russia's dirty intrigues are dragging us into this war; the Kaiser warned the Russians as late as 30th July. I still can't imagine what it's going to be like—putting the Russians, and hopefully the British Navy, in their places.

3. How useful is **Source A** as evidence of international tensions before the outbreak of World War One?

    4

Source B is part of a speech made by David Lloyd George in 1914.

Source B

> Have you heard the Kaiser's speeches? They are full of the bluster of German militarism, full of phrases like "mailed fist" and "shining armour". There is the same swagger and boastfulness running through every speech. He says "let us trample the Russians who challenge the supremacy of Germany in Europe and let us defeat Britain and take control of the seas! What will then be left?—nothing will be left except Germany:– 'Deutschland uber Alles'."

4. How far do **Sources A** and **B** disagree about the causes of World War One?

    5

[END OF CONTEXT IIB]

Marks

UNIT II—INTERNATIONAL COOPERATION AND CONFLICT

CONTEXT C: 1930s–1960s

SECTION A: KNOWLEDGE AND UNDERSTANDING

> At first the war had little effect upon people living in Germany.

1. Explain why the Second World War increasingly affected the lives of German civilians.   **4**

> The Charter of the United Nations Organisation was signed on August 4th, 1945.

2. Describe the difficulties faced by the United Nations in keeping international peace between 1945 and 1960.   **4**

SECTION B: ENQUIRY SKILLS

The following sources are about the Munich Conference during the Czech crisis of 1938.

**Study the sources carefully and answer the questions which follow.
You should use your own knowledge where appropriate.**

Source A is from a speech by Neville Chamberlain in the House of Commons in September 1938.

Source A

> The real triumph is that it has shown that four great powers can find it possible to agree on a way of carrying out a difficult operation by discussion instead of force of arms. The relief at our escape from war has, I think, everywhere been mingled in this country with a profound feeling of sympathy for Czechoslovakia. I have nothing to feel ashamed of. The path which leads to appeasement is long and full of obstacles. The question of Czechoslovakia is the latest and perhaps the most dangerous. Now that we have passed it, I feel it may be possible to make further progress along the road to sanity.

3. How useful is **Source A** as evidence about the agreement reached at Munich in 1938?   **4**

Source B is from a speech made by Winston Churchill in the House of Commons in October 1938.

Source B

> I will begin by saying that (Neville Chamberlain) has sustained a total and unmitigated defeat. All the hopes of a long peace which lay before Europe at the beginning of 1933, when Hitler came to power, and all the opportunities of stopping the growth of Nazi power, have been thrown away. So far as this country is concerned, the responsibility must rest with those who have control of our political affairs. And do not suppose that this is the end; this is only the beginning of the reckoning.

4. How far do **Sources A** and **B** disagree about the achievements of Neville Chamberlain?   **5**

[END OF CONTEXT IIC]

[Turn over for Unit III on *Page twelve*]

UNIT III—PEOPLE AND POWER

> ### CONTEXT A: USA 1850–1880

SECTION A: KNOWLEDGE AND UNDERSTANDING

> After the Civil War, the emancipated slaves of the South expected to become fully-fledged United States citizens.

(Note: for this answer you should write a short essay of several paragraphs including an introduction and a conclusion.)

1. How far would you agree that the most important problem facing Blacks in the South after the Civil War was:

   EITHER

   (*a*) the activities of the Ku Klux Klan?   **8**

   OR

   (*b*) the restrictions of the Black Codes?   **8**

SECTION B: ENQUIRY SKILLS

The following sources are about Westward expansion and its effect on the Native Americans.

**Study the sources carefully and answer the questions which follow.
You should use your own knowledge where appropriate.**

Source A is from a speech made by the Native American chief, Geronimo, to officials of the Government of the USA.

Source A

> We are held on lands which are not suited to our needs. Our people are decreasing in numbers here, and will continue to decrease unless they are allowed to return to their native land. There is no climate or soil which is equal to our previous home: the land which the Almighty created for us. I want to die in peace feeling that our numbers will not diminish as at present and that our name will not become extinct.

2. Discuss the attitude of the author of **Source A** towards the Government's treatment of the Native Americans.

   3

Marks

Source B is taken from "The American West" by Mike Mellor.

Source B

> After the Battle of Little Bighorn there was no prospect of a Native American military victory against the Whites. The only option for the Plains Indians was life on a reservation. They were given small amounts of land that white people did not want. They found this hard to accept as they were hunters, not farmers. Most of the Government agents were unsympathetic to the Native Americans. Food rations were often inadequate, as were medical supplies and disease killed many. Efforts were made to destroy their culture.

3. How far do **Sources A** and **B** agree about the Government's treatment of the Native Americans?

4

Source C is from a painting produced in 1849.

Source C

4. How fully does **Source C** show conditions for miners during the 1849 Gold Rush?

You should use **evidence from the source** and **your own knowledge** and give reasons for your answer.

5

[END OF CONTEXT IIIA]

Marks

UNIT III—PEOPLE AND POWER

CONTEXT B: INDIA 1917–1947

SECTION A: KNOWLEDGE AND UNDERSTANDING

> Prime Minister Attlee appointed Lord Mountbatten to deal with all the problems involved in getting Britain out of India.

(Note: for this answer you should write a short essay of several paragraphs, including an introduction and a conclusion.)

1. How far do you agree that the most important problem facing Mountbatten was:

EITHER

(*a*) achieving Indian independence?

8

OR

(*b*) dealing with the difficulties of partition?

8

SECTION B: ENQUIRY SKILLS

The following sources are about Mahatma Gandhi and Indian opposition to British rule.

**Study the sources carefully and answer the questions, which follow.
You should also use your own knowledge where appropriate.**

Source A was written by Arvind Nehra, an Indian who had been educated in England.

Source A

> Gandhi's ideals are about as unattainable as those with which I left Cambridge University. I also had wanted to bring about a better understanding between Indian and British people. It had all seemed so easy at Cambridge. But it is not so. Gandhi insists that every Indian must do without foreign goods. They must wear only the native Khaddar cloth. I sat down and worked this out one night, only to discover, alas, that there would be something like three inches of Indian cotton cloth per head of population.

2. Discuss the attitude of the author in **Source A** towards Gandhi's beliefs.

3

Marks

Source B is from "History of the Freedom Movement in India" by R. Majumdar.

Source B

> Gandhi's personality and saintly character inspired confidence. His will and enthusiasm alone stirred the masses into action. Gandhi always had a profound attraction to the Indian mind. His ideals and wishes appealed to everyone in a manner perhaps unique in the world's history. He could exploit a spirit of blind devotion and complete obedience in every Indian—to an extent usually reserved for a spiritual guru. Whatever sacrifice he asked of the Indians was accepted.

3. How far do **Sources A** and **B** agree about Gandhi and his beliefs?

4

Source C is a photograph from an Indian newspaper published in 1928.

Source C

4. How fully does **Source C** show Indian opposition to British rule in India in the 1920s?

You should use **evidence from the source** and **your own knowledge** and give reasons for your answer.

5

[*END OF CONTEXT IIIB*]

Marks

UNIT III—PEOPLE AND POWER

CONTEXT C: Russia 1914–1941

SECTION A: KNOWLEDGE AND UNDERSTANDING

Stalin wanted to stay in power and change Russia.

(Note: for this answer you must write a short essay of several paragraphs, including an introduction and a conclusion.)

1. How far would you agree that the most important method Stalin used to control Russia was:

   EITHER

   (*a*) the Five Year Plans?   **8**

   OR

   (*b*) the Purges?   **8**

SECTION B: ENQUIRY SKILLS

The following sources are about the effects of the rule of Tsar Nicholas II in Russia.

**Study the sources carefully and answer the questions which follow.
You should also use your own knowledge where appropriate.**

Source A is from the British Ambassador in Russia to the British Government in the early months of 1914.

Source A

Russia under Tsar Nicholas has had many problems. However, Russia is rapidly becoming powerful and is now stronger than at any time since the start of the century. The recent policies of the government have seen its metal-producing industry overtake that of Austria. Russia is now also producing thousands of tons of coal. Rapid industrialisation has led to the building of some enormous factories in St. Petersburg and Moscow. We must retain at all costs the friendship of the Tsar's great Empire.

---

2. Discuss the attitude of the author of **Source A** towards the Russia ruled by Tsar Nicholas.   **3**

Marks

Source B is from "Modern World History" by Ben Walsh.

Source B

> Tsar Nicholas was keen to see Russia becoming an industrial power. Policies were introduced which led to rapid industrial growth. Coal production trebled and, even more spectacularly, iron production quadrupled. Some peasants left the land to work in these new industries in cities: the heaviest concentrations being in Moscow and St. Petersburg. However, their living conditions hardly improved and other nations looked with horror at the poverty which existed in the Tsar's Russia.

3. How far do **Sources A** and **B** agree about the impact of the Tsar's rule on Russia?

4

Source C is a poster of discontented Russians during the time of Tsar Nicholas II. The Russian word used in the poster says "Bread".

Source C

„Хлеба"

4. How fully does **Source C** show discontent among Russian people in 1914?

You should use **evidence from the source** and **your own knowledge** and give reasons for your answer.

5

[*END OF CONTEXT IIIC*]

Marks

homework monday

UNIT III—PEOPLE AND POWER

CONTEXT D: Germany 1918–1939

SECTION A: KNOWLEDGE AND UNDERSTANDING

> The Nazis faced relatively little open opposition during their twelve years in power.

(Note: for this answer you should write a short essay of several paragraphs, including an introduction and a conclusion.)

1. How far would you agree that the main reason that opposition groups in Nazi Germany failed was:

EITHER

(*a*) the weaknesses of the opposition groups?　　8

OR

(*b*) the powers of the Nazi state?　　8

SECTION B: ENQUIRY SKILLS

The following sources are about the treatment of the Jews and young people in Nazi Germany.

**Study the sources carefully and answer the questions which follow.
You should also use your own knowledge where appropriate.**

Source A is from the diary of a German writer, Von Hassell, who was writing on November 25th, 1938.

Source A

> I am writing under the crushing emotion evoked by the evil persecution of the Jews after the murder of Von Rath. Not since the Great War have we lost so much credit in the world. Goebbels has seldom been so disbelieved as when he said that an unplanned outburst of anger among the people had caused the outrages. As a matter of fact, there is no doubt that we are dealing with an officially organised anti-Jewish riot which broke out at the same hour of night all over Germany.

2. Discuss the attitude of the author of **Source A** towards Nazi treatment of the Jews.　　3

Rachel

Marks

Source B is from a report by the American consul in Leipzig in November 1938.

Source B

> The attacks on Jewish property, which began in the early hours, were hailed subsequently in the Nazi press as a "spontaneous wave of righteous indignation throughout Germany, as a result of the cowardly Jewish murder of Von Rath". As far as many Germans are concerned, a state of popular indignation that would lead to such excesses can be considered as non-existent. On the contrary, all of the local crowd I observed were obviously stunned over what had happened and horrified over the unprecedented fury of the Nazi acts.

3. To what extent do **Sources A** and **B** agree about attacks on the Jews?   4

Source C is a photograph showing young girls at a Nazi rally in Coburg in the 1930s.

Source C

4. How fully does **Source C** show the extent of Nazi control of young people in the 1930s?

You should use **evidence from the source** and **your own knowledge** and give reasons for your answer.   5

[END OF UNIT IIID]

[END OF QUESTION PAPER]

[BLANK PAGE]

[BLANK PAGE]

G

1540/402

| NATIONAL QUALIFICATIONS 2006 | MONDAY, 15 MAY 10.20 AM – 11.50 AM | HISTORY STANDARD GRADE General Level |

Answer questions from Unit I **and** Unit II **and** Unit III.

Choose only **one** Context from each Unit and answer Sections A **and** B. The Contexts chosen should be those you have studied.

The Contexts in each Unit are:

Use the information in the sources, and your own knowledge, to answer the questions.

Number the questions as shown in the question paper.

Some sources have been adapted or translated.

SCOTTISH QUALIFICATIONS AUTHORITY

PB 1540/402 6/28570

Marks

UNIT I—CHANGING LIFE IN SCOTLAND AND BRITAIN

CONTEXT A: 1750s–1850s

SECTION A: KNOWLEDGE AND UNDERSTANDING

Study the information in the sources. You must also use your own knowledge in your answers.

Source A is from the New Statistical Account for Auchtertool in Fife, written in 1845.

Source A

> The state of farming is now very different to what it was 50 years ago. The new iron ploughs are generally used and the effects of these are visible in the state of the land when it receives the seed—now sown by machine. The progress of growth is greater—right up until the reaping. After the grain is ready for the barn, the use of threshing machines makes its preparation for the market speedy and easy.

1. Describe some new methods of farming the land in use by 1845.   **3**

Source B is from "The Oxford Companion to Scottish History".

Source B

> The famine of 1695–1699, when crops failed three years running, may have reduced the population of Scotland by 13%. Although it was the last nationwide famine, it was not the last period of hunger. With the coming of better farming however, such food shortages became rarer and the numbers dying of starvation dropped. People ate better and Scotland's population increased from about 1·25 million in 1755 to 2·9 million in 1851.

2. How important was a better food supply in causing Scotland's population to increase in the period 1750 to the 1850s?   **4**

Marks

SECTION B: ENQUIRY SKILLS

The issue for investigating is:

> The government was wrong to use force against the Radicals in Britain.

Study the sources carefully and answer the questions which follow.

You should use your own knowledge where appropriate.

Source C was written by Henry Cockburn, an Edinburgh lawyer, in his book "Memorials of Our Time".

Source C

> I remember the disturbances in 1819 and 1820 called "The Radical War". The whole country was suffering under great distress and many were out of work. This was taken advantage of by a few radicals who began to demand changes. There was a lot of excitement and some fighting. It was all exaggerated, however. The government said it was the start of a revolution and that the actions of some unhappy, unemployed weavers should be considered as a civil war. The government ordered soldiers to use force to stop the Radicals.

3. How useful is **Source C** for investigating government action against Radicals in the nineteenth century?   3

Source D is from "A History of the Scottish People" by T.C. Smout.

Source D

> In 1820 soldiers arrested 27 members of a Glasgow Radical Committee on suspicion that they were planning a revolution. On April 5th, the streets of Glasgow were lined with troops and there was a clash between 300 angry Radicals and some soldiers on horseback. A party of fifty Radicals left the town and marched towards Carron hoping to meet up with others and seize guns at the iron works. They were attacked by a group of soldiers and fled after a short fight in which four were wounded.

4. What evidence is there in **Source C** that the government should **not** have used force against the Radicals?

   What evidence in **Source D** suggests that the government were right to use force against the Radicals?   5

5. How far do you agree that the government was wrong to use force against the Radicals in Britain?

   You must use evidence **from the sources** and **your own knowledge** to come to a conclusion.   4

[END OF CONTEXT IA]

Now turn to the Context you have chosen in Unit II.

Marks

UNIT I—CHANGING LIFE IN SCOTLAND AND BRITAIN

CONTEXT B: 1830s–1930s

SECTION A: KNOWLEDGE AND UNDERSTANDING

Study the information in the sources. You must also use your own knowledge in your answers.

Source A was written by the historian Richard Fenton.

Source A

> By 1850 the shape of the fields as we know them today was established. Underground drains in use after 1850 replaced the need for surface drainage. The surfaces were now more level in the enclosed fields. This led to further crop improvements such as potatoes. It was also now easier to manage the different kinds of livestock. This made possible the quick adoption of new equipment with a resulting growth in farming toolmakers. These changes mainly took place in the Lowlands.

1. Describe some new methods of farming the land in use by the 1930s.   **3**

Source B is from "The Scottish Nation" by T.M. Devine.

Source B

> The increase in Scotland's urban population happened very quickly in the nineteenth century. The main reason for this growth was the revolution in agriculture. Population increase could not have taken place without a substantial increase in food production. The workers in the towns did not cultivate their own supplies. The urban working class relied on grain, milk, potatoes and meat supplied from Scottish farms. People ate better and the population increased from 2·3 million in 1831 to 4 million by 1891.

2. How important was an improved food supply in causing Scotland's population to increase in the period 1830–1930?   **4**

Marks

SECTION B: ENQUIRY SKILLS

The issue for investigating is:

> The government was right to use forceful action against the Suffragettes in Britain.

Study the sources carefully and answer the questions which follow.

You should use your own knowledge where appropriate.

Source C is from the "Daily Express" written in 1909.

Source C

> The Suffragettes' militant actions have gone too far. Politicians have been interrupted while making speeches. The Prime Minister has had his windows broken. Last year, we warned the government that the time for dealing gently with these mischievous women had ended. Those who call themselves militant Suffragettes need to be halted. These women who unite to create disorder deserve to be forcibly arrested. It is good to see the government now using its full force against the WSPU.

3. How useful is **Source C** for investigating government action against the Suffragettes?   3

Source D is from "Scotland and Britain 1830–1980" by S. Chalmers and L. Cheyne.

Source D

> In response to Suffragettes going on hunger strike, the government introduced force feeding, as they argued they could not let women die. Many people were horrified at the cruelty of the government. The government was condemned for its brutality to women. Force feeding was a dreadful, painful business. The bravery and determination of the women being force fed gained them the admiration of many people. It caused many men to take them more seriously. The General Election of 1910 showed the Liberal Government had lost a lot of support.

4. What evidence in **Source C** agrees with the government's use of forceful action against the Suffragettes?

   What evidence in **Source D** disagrees with the government's use of forceful action against the Suffragettes?   5

5. How far do you agree that the British government was right to use forceful action against the Suffragettes in Britain?

   You must use evidence **from the sources** and **your own knowledge** to come to a conclusion.   4

[END OF CONTEXT IB]

Now turn to the Context you have chosen in Unit II.

Marks

UNIT I—CHANGING LIFE IN SCOTLAND AND BRITAIN

CONTEXT C: 1880s–Present Day

SECTION A: KNOWLEDGE AND UNDERSTANDING

Study the information in the sources. You must also use your own knowledge in your answers.

Source A is about changes in women's employment since the Second World War.

Source A

> The development of a number of household gadgets that became more widely available from the 1950s greatly eased the burden of housework for women. Men increasingly have helped with household tasks, although in many households women are still expected to run the home and hold down a full-time job. Changes in industry created more jobs for women. Part-time work was increasingly available, which suited many women with young children.

1. Describe the changes which made it easier for women to go out to work after 1945.   **3**

Source B is from "British Social and Economic History" by Ben Walsh.

Source B

> By the 1880s, improvements in farming meant people enjoyed a better diet. Clean water helped to wipe out many of the killer diseases such as cholera and typhoid fever. By the 1930s, people were spending more money on fruit than on bread, which improved their health. A healthier diet increased people's resistance to disease. In more modern times, the risk of cancer and heart disease has been reduced through an improved diet.

2. How important was better diet as a reason for Scotland's population increasing after 1880?   **4**

SECTION B: ENQUIRY SKILLS

The issue for investigating is:

> The government was right to use forceful action against the Suffragettes in Britain.

Study the sources carefully and answer the questions which follow.

You should use your own knowledge where appropriate.

Source C is from the "Daily Express" written in 1909.

Source C

> The Suffragettes' militant action have gone too far. Politicians have been interrupted while making speeches. The Prime Minister has had his windows broken. Last year, we warned the government that the time for dealing gently with these mischievous women had ended. Those who call themselves militant Suffragettes need to be halted. These women who unite to create disorder deserve to be forcibly arrested. It is good to see the government now using its full force against the WSPU.

3. How useful is **Source C** for investigating government action against the Suffragettes?   **3**

Source D is from "Scotland and Britain 1830–1980" by S. Chalmers and L. Cheyne.

Source D

> In response to Suffragettes going on hunger strike, the government introduced force feeding, as they argued they could not let women die. Many people were horrified at the cruelty of the government. The government was condemned for its brutality to women. Force feeding was a dreadful, painful business. The bravery and determination of the women being force fed gained them the admiration of many people. It caused many men to take them more seriously. The General Election of 1910 showed the Liberal Government had lost a lot of support.

4. What evidence in **Source C** agrees with the government's use of forceful action against the Suffragettes?

   What evidence in **Source D** disagrees with the government's use of forceful action against the Suffragettes?   **5**

5. How far do you agree that the British government was right to use forceful action against the Suffragettes in Britain?

   You must use evidence **from the sources** and **your own knowledge** to come to a conclusion.   **4**

[END OF CONTEXT IC]

Now turn to the Context you have chosen in Unit II.

Marks

UNIT II—INTERNATIONAL COOPERATION AND CONFLICT

CONTEXT A: 1790s–1820s

SECTION A: KNOWLEDGE AND UNDERSTANDING

Study the information in the sources. You must also use your own knowledge in your answers.

Source A gives information about the Battle of Leipzig in October 1813.

Source A

	France	Allies of the Fourth Coalition
Commanded by	Napoleon	Schwarzenberg, Blucher, Bernadotte
Soldiers from	France, Poland, Germany	Austria, Russia, Prussia, Sweden
Size of armies	177,500	332,000
Losses	68,000	54,000

1. Describe the strengths of the Fourth Coalition in October 1813. **3**

Source B is from a letter written by Bernard Coleridge, aged 11, from his ship at sea, to his father.

Source B

> We live on beef which has been ten or eleven years stored in corn and on biscuits which quite make your throat cold owing to the maggots which are very cold when you eat them. We drink water of the colour of the bark of a tree and there are plenty of little weevils in it. Our wine is exactly like bullock's blood and sawdust mixed together. I hope I shall not learn to swear like the other sailors, and, with God's help, I shall not.

2. How important was poor diet as a cause of complaint on board ships in Nelson's navy? **3**

Marks

SECTION B: ENQUIRY SKILLS

The following sources are about Spain and the Congress System.

Study the sources carefully and answer the questions which follow.

You should use your own knowledge where appropriate.

Source C is part of a note sent by Metternich to the government of Spain in December 1822.

Source C

> The rulers of Austria, Prussia, Russia and France were unwilling to interfere in the internal affairs of Spain—if revolution could be kept inside Spanish territory. But this is not the case. The Revolution in Spain has been the cause of great disasters in other states. It was the Revolution which set the example for others in Naples and Piedmont. If the Congress powers had not become involved there would have been uprisings throughout Italy. France and Germany would also have been threatened.

3. How fully does **Source C** explain why the Congress powers interfered in events in Spain in the 1820s?

   You must use evidence **from the source** and **from your own knowledge** and give reasons for your answer.   4

Source D is a modern cartoon about the Congress System.

Source D

A FATAL TUG-OF-WAR.

Divisions among powers will spell the end of the Congress System.

4. What is the attitude of the author of **Source D** towards the Congress System?   3

[Turn over

Source E is from "Mastering Modern History" by Norman Lowe.

Source E

> One result of the Greek revolt was that it marked the end of the Congress System as an instrument for crushing revolutions. For the first time Russia was acting with Britain and France in opposition to Austria. There could be no further pretence that Europe was united. This suited British Foreign Secretary Canning who wanted to break up the Congress System for a number of reasons but mainly to further Britain's trading interests.

5. To what extent do **Sources D** and **E** agree about the problems facing the Congress System?

   4

[END OF CONTEXT IIA]

Now turn to the Context you have chosen in Unit III.

Marks

UNIT II—INTERNATIONAL COOPERATION AND CONFLICT

CONTEXT B: 1890s–1920s

SECTION A: KNOWLEDGE AND UNDERSTANDING

Study the information in the sources. You must also use your own knowledge in your answers.

Source A shows the strengths of the British and German navies in 1914.

Source A

	Britain	Germany
Dreadnoughts	20	13
Destroyers	301	144
Submarines	78	30

1. Describe the Arms Race in Europe in the years 1900–1914.　　　3

Source B is taken from "World History from 1914 to the Present Day" by C. Culpin.

Source B

> Aircraft were still new inventions in 1914, and the part they could play in war had not really been thought out. At first they were used for reconnaissance, to find out what the enemy was doing. The light spotter planes could fly over enemy lines to take photographs. Later, fighter planes were designed to shoot down enemy aircraft and protect the troops in the trenches. The Royal Flying Corps, which had been founded in April 1912, became the basis of the Royal Air Force.

2. How important a role did air technology play on the Western Front during the First World War?　　　3

[Turn over

Marks

SECTION B: ENQUIRY SKILLS

The following sources are about the League of Nations during the 1920s.

Study the sources carefully and answer the questions which follow.

You should use your own knowledge where appropriate.

Source C is a 1920s cartoon showing the League of Nations taking steps towards world peace across "shark-infested waters."

Source C

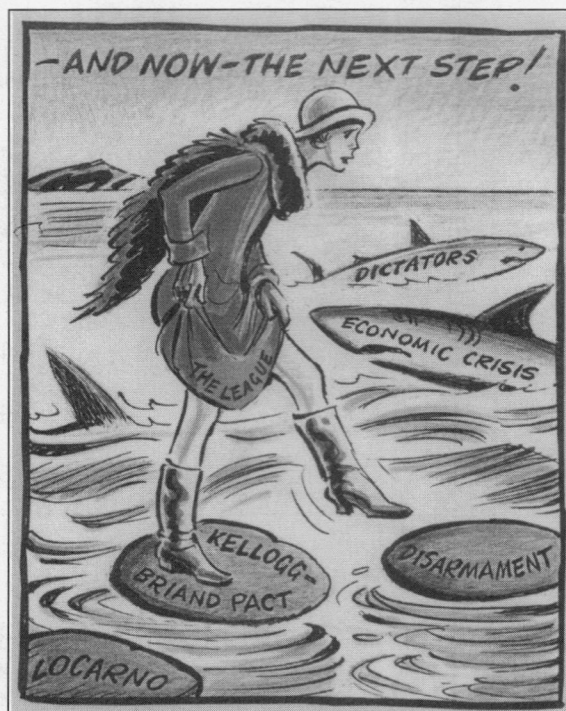

3. What is the attitude of the author of **Source C** towards the League of Nations' progress in achieving world peace?

3

Source D is taken from "The Struggle for Peace, 1918–1989" by J. Traynor.

Source D

> By 1928, ten years had gone by without a major war. Over sixty nations had sworn not to go to war as a means of settling their disputes. The next step forward would be disarmament. In such conditions of economic depression and suspicion, countries were less likely to work together on behalf of the League. A further problem was the rise of dictators in Europe, such as Mussolini in Italy. Dictators who had seized power by force were not likely to work with others to prevent war and for the peaceful ideals of the League.

4. How far do **Sources C** and **D** agree about the problems faced by the League of Nations in the 1920s?

4

Marks

Source E is taken from "Modern World History".

Source E

> The setting up of the League of Nations was written into the Treaty of Versailles. Refugees fleeing from conflicts were given vital help. A famous Norwegian explorer, Fridjof Nansen, worked for the League on the problems of prisoners of war stranded in Russia and he helped half a million men to return safely home. The Health Organisation organised work on health matters, especially in poorer countries. It worked successfully to reduce the number of cases of leprosy. The absence of the USA, however, greatly weakened the authority of the League.

5. How fully does **Source E** show the successes of the League of Nations during the 1920s?

   You must use evidence **from the source** and **from your own knowledge** and give reasons for your answer. 4

[END OF CONTEXT IIB]

Now turn to the Context you have chosen in Unit III.

[BLANK PAGE]

Marks

UNIT II—INTERNATIONAL COOPERATION AND CONFLICT

CONTEXT C: 1930s–1960s

SECTION A: KNOWLEDGE AND UNDERSTANDING

Study the information in the sources. You must also use your own knowledge in your answers.

Source A shows the growth of the German navy and air force in the 1930s.

Source A

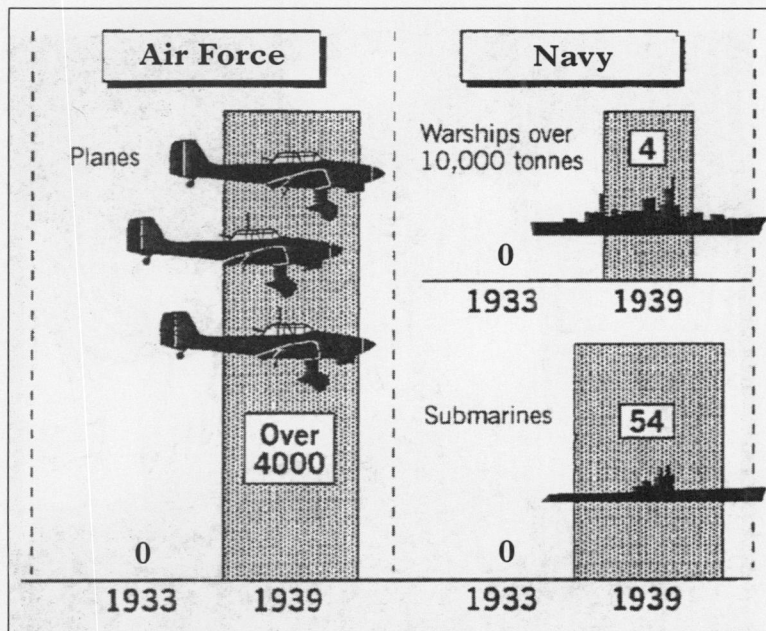

1. In what ways did Hitler increase Germany's military strength between 1933 and 1939? **3**

Source B is from "International Cooperation and Conflict" by W. Doran and R. Dargie.

Source B

> In 1956 there was a revolution in Cuba where Fidel Castro became the new President. In 1962 United States spy-planes took photographs of Soviet missile launchers in Cuba. President Kennedy thought the Soviet Union was preparing to attack the USA and his advisers urged him to bomb the bases in Cuba.

2. How important was the Cuban Missile Crisis in causing international tension in the early 1960s?

3

[Turn over

Marks

SECTION B: ENQUIRY SKILLS

The following sources are about the United Nations.

Study the sources carefully and answer the questions which follow.

You should use your own knowledge where appropriate.

Source C is a cartoon about the United Nations. The three soldiers are from the UN's biggest members—USA, Britain and the Soviet Union.

Source C

"And now let's learn to live together"

3. What is the attitude of the author of **Source C** towards the role of the United Nations?   **3**

Marks

Source D is from the Charter of the United Nations.

Source D

> We, the peoples of the United Nations, are determined to save succeeding generations from the scourge of war. Twice in our lifetime it has brought untold sorrow to mankind. We aim to develop friendly relations among nations and settle disputes peacefully. We aim to promote better standards of living everywhere in the world. We promise to practise tolerance and live together in peace with one another as good neighbours.

4. How far do **Sources C** and **D** agree about the role of the United Nations?   **4**

Source E is from "Our World Today" by Derek Heater.

Source E

> Although it has tried to live up to the proud aims of its Charter, since the United Nations was formed in 1945, the world has become a much more dangerous place. Many wars have been fought and there are thousands of nuclear weapons now in the world. The UN has been powerless to stop all of this. Some reports also claim that some officials are inefficient and waste a lot of money.

5. How fully does **Source E** describe the problems of the United Nations?

   You must use evidence **from the source** and **from your own knowledge** and give reasons for your answer.   **4**

[END OF CONTEXT IIC]

Now turn to the Context you have chosen in Unit III.

Marks

UNIT III—PEOPLE AND POWER

CONTEXT A: USA 1850–1880

SECTION A: KNOWLEDGE AND UNDERSTANDING

Study the information in the sources. You must also use your own knowledge in your answers.

Source A describes what happened when Abraham Lincoln was elected president.

Source A

> The Southern reaction to Lincoln's election was quick and decisive. Within three months of the election—before Lincoln was even sworn in—seven Southern states seceded from the Union and formed the Confederate States of America. In all, eleven states would eventually join the Confederacy.

1. Describe the events that happened after Lincoln's election as President.   **3**

Source B is about the Mormons.

Source B

> The Mormons went West to escape persecution. Ordinary people were irritated by the Mormons' hard work and carefulness. Rumours of the existence of a Mormon secret society called the Danites added to their fears. Most of the Mormon leaders were imprisoned. Non-Mormons were disgusted when they found out Mormon men could have more than one wife at the same time. This led to fears that there would be a Mormon population explosion and they would be outnumbered.

2. Explain why many Americans disliked the Mormons in the period 1850–1880.   **4**

SECTION B: ENQUIRY SKILLS

The following sources are about the Freedmen's Bureau.

Study the sources carefully and answer the questions which follow.

You should use your own knowledge where appropriate.

Source C was written by the historian, Hugh Brogan.

Source C

> The Freedmen's Bureau was set up by Congress in 1865 and did heroic work in providing homes and food for former slaves. Despite much opposition in the South, it succeeded in establishing 4,000 schools. It also improved health facilities by setting up 100 hospitals. The Freedmen's Bureau also protected ex-slaves by supervising the terms under which they were hired as free men. However, its officials were resented by the Ku Klux Klan particularly when the Bureau took plantation owners to court for breaking new labour contracts.

3. What is the attitude of the author of **Source C** towards the work of the Freedmen's Bureau?

3

Source D is taken from "Black Peoples of the Americas" by Bob Rees and Marika Sherwood.

Source D

> In 1865 Congress set up Freedmen's Bureau to help Blacks get employment and civil rights after the Civil War ended. It had opened 100 hospitals and operated over 4,000 primary schools. Food was given to the poorest Blacks and Whites. The Freedmen's Bank was also opened. Such new opportunities were quickly seized by ex-slaves but alarmed Southern Whites in organisations like the Ku Klux Klan.

4. How far do **Sources C** and **D** agree about the work of the Freedmen's Bureau?

4

[END OF CONTEXT IIIA]

Marks

UNIT III—PEOPLE AND POWER

CONTEXT B: INDIA 1917–1947

SECTION A: KNOWLEDGE AND UNDERSTANDING

Study the information in the sources. You must also use your own knowledge in your answers.

Source A was written by Professor Niall Ferguson.

Source A

> General Dyer's actions in the Amritsar massacre were harsh. The event produced martyrs for the Indian nationalist cause. It also created a crisis of confidence in Britain. Nationalist grievances were growing strongly in India. The British Empire had been shaken. In previous centuries the British had felt no concerns about shooting to kill. That had started to change. The ruthless determination to defend the Empire seemed to have vanished.

  1. Describe the results of the Amritsar massacre of April 1919.   **3**

Source B is from the Indian politician Nehru's autobiography written in 1941.

Source B

> I returned to India after some travels in Europe. When I first read about Gandhi's Satyaghraha (non violence) in the newspapers, I was very relieved. Here at last was a way out of our difficulties with the British. This was a method of action which was open and possibly effective. When we later saw the organised enthusiasm of the people during the Salt Campaign, we felt ashamed for doubting Gandhi. We marvelled at the ways in which salt making was spreading.

  2. Explain why Gandhi's campaign tactics for independence attracted support from Indians.   **4**

Marks

SECTION B: ENQUIRY SKILLS

The following sources are views on Indian independence.

Study the sources carefully and answer the questions which follow.

You should use your own knowledge where appropriate.

Source C shows the views of Hugh Dalton, an important member of the Labour Government after World War Two.

Source C

> The Congress Party and Gandhi have been for many years pushing hard for Indian independence. Indians have supported the war effort in huge numbers. We have not given a great deal to the Indian people. We are in a place where Indians shout aloud that we are not wanted. We do not have the military force to squash those Indians who don't want us ruling India. The only thing to do is to get out.

3. What are Hugh Dalton's views, as shown in **Source C**, on Indian independence?   **3**

Source D is from "Britain in the World since 1945" by John Ray.

Source D

> There had been many difficult times since 1939. There were some people in Britain who said that India should never be given up. Trade with India had brought so much wealth to Britain. India had been called "the brightest jewel in the British crown". The British had ruled there for two centuries during which time they had built roads and railways. They had taken education and medicine to Indians. The British Empire still had the power to control millions of people across all continents.

4. How far do **Sources C** and **D** disagree on whether Britain should have given India its independence?   **4**

[END OF CONTEXT IIIB]

Marks

UNIT III—PEOPLE AND POWER

CONTEXT C: RUSSIA 1914–1941

SECTION A: KNOWLEDGE AND UNDERSTANDING

Study the information in the sources. You must also use your own knowledge in your answers.

Source A is from "Romanov to Gorbachev" by Peter Mantin and Colin Lankester.

Source A

> The main feature of the revolution in February 1917, was that it was not planned but took everyone by surprise. It had no leaders and therefore there was no one ready to take the leadership of the country. As a result, the leaders of the Duma were forced to take charge of the country. The leader of the Petrograd Soviet, Alexander Kerensky, became Minister of Justice. This gave the Soviet some direct say in the running of the country. In effect, the Provisional Government and the Petrograd Soviet formed a "Dual Government" which ruled Russia.

1. Describe the results of the February Revolution in 1917.   **3**

Source B is from "Reaction and Revolutions: Russia 1881–1924" by Michael Lynch.

Source B

> In the final assessment, the outstanding factor explaining the success of the Reds in the Civil War was their clear sense of purpose. By contrast, the Whites were an uncoordinated collection of separate forces, whose morale was never high. Since they were without a common cause, other than hatred of Reds, the Whites lacked effective leadership. This was a problem they were unable to resolve. No White leader emerged of the ability of Trotsky or Lenin.

2. Explain why the Whites lost the Civil War.   **4**

Marks

SECTION B: ENQUIRY SKILLS

The following sources are about the treatment of the Kulaks.

Study the sources carefully and answer the questions which follow.

You should use your own knowledge where appropriate.

Source C is from a speech made by Joseph Stalin in December 1929.

Source C

> Now we are able to carry on a determined offensive against the Kulaks, break their resistance to collectivisation, eliminate them as a class and replace their output by the output of the collective farms. Now, the elimination of the Kulaks is being carried out by the masses of poor and middle peasants themselves. They are putting complete collectivisation into practice. There is another question: whether the Kulaks should be allowed to join the collective farms? Of course not, for they are the sworn enemies of the collective farm movement.

3. What is the attitude of Stalin in **Source C** towards the Kulaks?   3

Source D is from Y. Kukushkin, a Soviet historian.

Source D

> The Kulaks were resisting the collective farm movement in a bid to retain their positions, cost what it might. The Kulaks began to wage a campaign of terror against those who supported and worked for collectivisation. In late 1927 and early 1928, the Kulaks everywhere began to refuse to sell their produce at state-fixed prices. They hid grain and sabotaged the grain trade in a bid to destabilise the socialist economy. The increasingly serious class struggle in the countryside made the liquidation of the Kulaks as a class a top priority task.

4. How far do **Sources C** and **D** agree about the Kulaks and collectivisation?   4

[END OF CONTEXT IIIC]

Marks

UNIT III—PEOPLE AND POWER

CONTEXT D: GERMANY 1918–1939

SECTION A: KNOWLEDGE AND UNDERSTANDING

Study the information in the sources. You must also use your own knowledge in your answers.

Source A is from "Germany 1918–39" by John Kerr.

Source A

> In 1923, the Nazis attempted to seize power in Munich and overthrow the Bavarian Government. With the collapse of this Beer Hall Putsch, most people believed that Hitler and the Nazis were finished. But the trial gave Hitler much needed national publicity. He was photographed standing beside Ludendorff which made people think that Hitler was an important person. When he was found guilty, Hitler was given a short prison sentence.

1. Describe the results of the Beer Hall Putsch, 1923.   **3**

Source B is a modern historian's view of the "Night of the Long Knives".

Source B

> By 1934, the SA "bully boys" had outlived their usefulness to Hitler. He acted swiftly and without warning. On June 30th, SA leaders were arrested and immediately shot. Ernst Roehm, the SA leader, was among the many victims. Hitler justified his actions on the grounds that Roehm was plotting to overthrow the government. The episode not only removed some of Hitler's opponents, it also showed would-be opponents that Hitler was ready to act ruthlessly whenever threatened.

2. Explain why Hitler was able to defeat his opponents in the 1930s.   **4**

Marks

SECTION B: ENQUIRY SKILLS

The following sources are about attitudes in Germany towards National Socialism.

Study the sources carefully and answer the questions which follow.

You should use your own knowledge where appropriate.

Source C is from the memories of Karl Billinger, a German Communist, published in 1935.

Source C

> For three months after the Nazis came to power, I managed to avoid saluting the swastika flag. You could always steer clear of SA parades and demonstrations by turning off into a side street. I tried it once too often, however. I caught sight of an approaching procession and without thinking I turned my back on it and walked away. Four Brown Shirt thugs crossed towards me and one said. "Are you trying to get out of it? Salute! Now!" I did this and said "Heil Hitler". I could have spat at myself as I walked past the procession with my arm in the air.

3. What was the attitude of the author of **Source C** towards the Nazis?   **3**

Source D was written by historians G. Lacey and K. Shepherd.

Source D

> At first many people refused to join the Nazi Party. Some did not give the "Heil Hitler" salute. All the evidence suggests that ordinary Germans greatly resented many aspects of the Nazi regime such as the strong-arm tactics of the SA. As for the endless meetings and parades, even by the end of the 1933 these were treated with indifference by many. People attended because their jobs might depend on it. Grumbling became a national pastime—but it was rarely done in public.

4. How far do **Sources C** and **D** agree on attitudes in Germany towards the Nazis?   **4**

[END OF CONTEXT IIID]

[END OF QUESTION PAPER]

[BLANK PAGE]

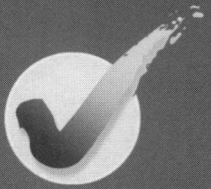

[BLANK PAGE]

[BLANK PAGE]

C

1540/403

NATIONAL
QUALIFICATIONS
2006

MONDAY, 15 MAY
1.00 PM – 2.45 PM

HISTORY
STANDARD GRADE
Credit Level

Answer questions from Unit I **and** Unit II **and** Unit III.

Choose only **one** Context from each Unit and answer Sections A **and** B. The Contexts chosen should be those you have studied.

The Contexts in each Unit are:

Number the questions as shown in the question paper.

Some sources have been adapted or translated.

SCOTTISH
QUALIFICATIONS
AUTHORITY

©

Marks

UNIT I—CHANGING LIFE IN SCOTLAND AND BRITAIN

CONTEXT A: 1750s–1850s

SECTION A: KNOWLEDGE AND UNDERSTANDING

> The inhabitants of Edinburgh chose to build houses close to the protection of the Castle and this resulted in high tenement buildings.

1. Describe some of the problems of living in high rise accommodation in the early nineteenth century.   **3**

> By the late eighteenth century, as a result of the new technology, successful mills had been established in places like New Lanark and Blantyre.

2. Explain some of the ways in which new technology affected the textile industry in the late eighteenth century.   **4**

SECTION B: ENQUIRY SKILLS

The issue for investigating is:

> Emigration from the Highlands and Islands of Scotland in the nineteenth century was beneficial for the emigrants.

**Study the sources carefully and answer the questions which follow.
You should use your own knowledge where appropriate.**

Source A was written in 1851 by Francis Clark, the owner of the Island of Ulva, in a report on Highland poverty.

Source A

> When it no longer became profitable to collect kelp (seaweed) I still paid my tenants to collect it — or they would have had no money at all. Farming cannot be well done on the island as the soil is poor and the weather uncertain. To make some money for myself I have been converting some crofts into farms for sheep. I have increased my sheep stock as the removal of crofters gave me more space. The population of Ulva was 500; it is now 150. Some went to other parts of Scotland but most went to America, Australia or Canada where they are doing well.

3. How useful is **Source A** for investigating emigration from the Highlands and Islands of Scotland in the nineteenth century?   **4**

Marks

Source B is from an eyewitness account from Catherine MacPhee of Barra in 1836.

Source B

> I saw our houses swept away and the people being driven out of the countryside to the streets of Glasgow and to the wilds of Canada, such as them that did not die of hunger and smallpox while going across the ocean. I have seen the women putting their children in the carts which were being sent from Benbecula to board an emigrant ship on Loch Boisdale. Almost everyone was crying. Bailiffs and constables gathered behind them and made sure they boarded the ship. Some men showed boldness and looked for adventure but for most it was a loathsome day.

Source C is from a letter written by John Scott in Ontario, Canada, to his uncle in Scotland in 1835.

Source C

> We had a good journey out on a new ship with few passengers. I am building a new house and a barn. This is a wild country but we have managed with great difficulty to chop down about seven acres of trees. We ripped out the stumps using levers as we had no oxen to pull them out. All the livestock we have now is a sow and a male pig but we are hoping to do well in this new land.

Look at Sources A, B and C.

4. What evidence is there in the sources to support the view that emigration was beneficial for emigrants from the Highlands and Islands of Scotland?

    What evidence in the sources disagrees with the view that emigration was beneficial for emigrants from the Highlands and Islands of Scotland?   **6**

5. How far do you agree that emigration from the Highlands and Islands of Scotland in the nineteenth century was beneficial for the emigrants?

    You must use evidence **from the sources** and **your own knowledge** to reach a **balanced conclusion**.   **5**

[END OF CONTEXT IA]

Marks

UNIT I—CHANGING LIFE IN SCOTLAND AND BRITAIN

> ### CONTEXT B: 1830s–1930s

SECTION A: KNOWLEDGE AND UNDERSTANDING

> In many Scottish towns tenement buildings were built as it was cheaper to build upwards rather than outwards.

1. Describe some of the problems of living in tenement accommodation before 1914.   **3**

> By the 1930s coal production in some Scottish areas had improved as a result of technological changes.

2. Explain some of the ways in which new technology affected the coal industry before the 1930s.   **4**

SECTION B: ENQUIRY SKILLS

The issue for investigating is:

> Emigration from the Highlands and Islands of Scotland between 1830 and 1930 was beneficial for the emigrants.

Study the sources carefully and answer the questions which follow.
You should use your own knowledge where appropriate.

Source A was written by a journalist from Fife in his "Notes of a Winter Tour of the Highlands" in 1847.

Source A

> The most vivid description would not do justice to the extraordinary and disgusting filth of Roag near Dunvegan. The people barricade themselves up behind their cows in the farthest and smallest end of the hut. There the whole family sits in dirt, and smoke, and darkness. They stare from morning to night into a peat fire. They appear quite contented to have no clean air or clean water. They must be instructed, and assisted to escape these conditions, and encouraged to emigrate.

3. How useful is **Source A** for investigating emigration from the Highlands and Islands of Scotland in the period 1830–1930?   **4**

Marks

Source B is from an eyewitness account from Catherine MacPhee of Barra in 1836.

Source B

> I saw our houses swept away and the people being driven out of the countryside to the streets of Glasgow and to the wilds of Canada, such as them that did not die of hunger and smallpox while going across the ocean. I have seen the women putting their children in the carts which were being sent from Benbecula to board an emigrant ship on Loch Boisdale. Almost everyone was crying. Bailiffs and constables gathered behind them and made sure they boarded the ship. Some men showed boldness and looked for adventure but for most if was a loathsome day.

Source C is from the memoirs of John MacDonald who emigrated from Uist to Canada in 1912.

Source C

> We settled in British Columbia, on the west coast of Canada. Many Scots emigrated because of the better living prospects that life in Canada offered them. Unlike some emigrants, we had no difficulty settling down as we had two uncles and an aunt to welcome us. Scottish emigrants received a special warm welcome from the Canadians. I met hundreds of Scottish, mainly Highland, emigrants in Vancouver. All of our family in Canada stayed on at school till they were fourteen. None of us regretted leaving Uist.

Look at Sources A, B and C.

4. What evidence is there in the sources to support the view that emigration was beneficial for emigrants from the Highlands and Islands of Scotland?

   What evidence in the sources disagrees with the view that emigration was beneficial for emigrants from the Highlands and Islands of Scotland?   **6**

5. How far do you agree that emigration from the Highlands and Islands of Scotland between 1830 and 1930 was beneficial for the emigrants?

   You must use evidence **from the sources** and **your own knowledge** to reach a **balanced conclusion**.   **5**

[END OF CONTEXT IB]

Marks

UNIT I—CHANGING LIFE IN SCOTLAND AND BRITAIN

CONTEXT C: 1880s–Present Day

SECTION A: KNOWLEDGE AND UNDERSTANDING

> All the cities began to build blocks of high-rise flats. Glasgow, especially, developed this form of housing.

1. Describe some of the problems of living in high-rise flats after 1950. **3**

> Car ownership in Scotland increased but there were different views on whether this was really an improvement.

2. Explain some of the ways in which motor transport affected the lives of people in Scotland in the twentieth century. **4**

SECTION B: ENQUIRY SKILLS

The issue for investigating is:

> Emigration from Scotland after 1880 was beneficial for the emigrants.

**Study the sources carefully and answer the questions which follow.
You should use your own knowledge where appropriate.**

Source A is from the memoirs of John MacDonald, a Highlander who emigrated from Uist to Canada in 1912.

Source A

> We settled in British Columbia, on the west coast of Canada. Many Scots emigrated because of the better living prospects that life in Canada offered them. Unlike some emigrants, we had no difficulty settling down as we had two uncles and an aunt to welcome us. Scottish emigrants received a special warm welcome from the Canadians. I met hundreds of Scottish, mainly Highland, emigrants in Vancouver. All of our family in Canada stayed on at school till they were fourteen. None of us regretted leaving Uist.

3. How useful is **Source A** for investigating emigration from Scotland after 1880? **4**

Marks

Source B is from Bibby's Quarterly, a magazine for British farmers, published in May 1899.

Source B

> Many people have been persuaded to leave by the exaggerated claims of emigration agents. They contrast the poverty and hardship in Britain with the greater freedom and wealth overseas. By telling such lies, thousands have been encouraged to leave comfortable homes and good friends but at the end of their journey they have found hostile land and crowded cities. We know many individuals and families who have emigrated and who have returned home, after great expense and loss of time.

Source C is from "Expansion, Trade and Industry" by Christopher Culpin, published in 1993.

Source C

> Huge numbers of people left Britain, some for "push" reasons and others for "pull" reasons. The "push" reasons included the terrible living conditions many workers faced. Poor wages made life a hard struggle to survive. The "pull" reasons were the opportunities for a better future offered by Australia, Canada and America. Some emigrants were attracted by the promise of cheap farmland. Although improvements in ships made the emigrants' journey safer and easier, they still suffered considerable hardships on the long voyages.

Look at Sources A, B and C

4. What evidence is there in the sources to support the view that emigration was beneficial for emigrants from Scotland?

   What evidence in the sources disagrees with the view that emigration was beneficial for emigrants from Scotland?　　6

5. How far do you agree that emigration from Scotland after 1880 was beneficial for the emigrants?

   You must use evidence **from the sources** and **your own knowledge** to reach a **balanced conclusion**.　　5

[END OF CONTEXT IC]

Marks

UNIT II—INTERNATIONAL COOPERATION AND CONFLICT

CONTEXT A: 1790s–1820s

SECTION A: KNOWLEDGE AND UNDERSTANDING

> The execution of Louis XVI was the final challenge to the rest of Europe.

1. How important was the death of Louis XVI as a cause of war between Britain and France?   **5**

> There was now, in 1815, the chance of a long and lasting peace with France.

2. Describe how France was treated in the Vienna Settlement, following the Hundred Days.   **4**

SECTION B: ENQUIRY SKILLS

The following sources are about the effects of war on the civilian populations in Britain and in France.

**Study the sources carefully and answer the questions which follow.
You should use your own knowledge where appropriate.**

Source A is a French cartoon showing the intended effects of the Continental System upon Britain. It was produced in 1806.

Source A

3. How useful is **Source A** as evidence of the effects of war on civilians in Britain?   **4**

Marks

Source B is from an address made by members of the French Senate in December 1813.

Source B

> Our ills are now at their height. We are suffering from poverty unexampled in the whole history of the state. Commerce is destroyed; industry is dying. What are the causes of these unutterable miseries? The answer is a government which causes excessive taxes and creates deplorable methods for their collection; a government which practises cruel methods of recruiting for the armies. The barbarous and endless war swallows up the youth of the country and tears them from education, agriculture and commerce.

4. Discuss the attitude of the authors of **Source B** towards the government in France in 1813.

3

Source C is from "Britain 1714–1851" by Denis Richards and Anthony Quick.

Source C

> By 1797 Britain had weathered the storm of financial crisis. This was partly due to the introduction of a form of income tax. However, though the country came through its dangers, the distress among the poorer classes was now acute. The war sent food prices soaring but wages made no corresponding advance, especially in country districts in the South. For many, starvation loomed ahead. The main effect of the French Revolution, it seemed, was to involve Britain in a lengthy war which needed vast amounts of young manpower.

5. To what extent do **Sources B** and **C** agree about the effects of the war on civilians in Britain and France?

5

[END OF CONTEXT IIA]

UNIT II—INTERNATIONAL COOPERATION AND CONFLICT

CONTEXT B: 1890s–1920s

SECTION A: KNOWLEDGE AND UNDERSTANDING

> The event which finally triggered war came on 28th June 1914 in Sarajevo, a town in the Austro-Hungarian province of Bosnia.

1. How important were the assassinations of the Archduke Franz Ferdinand and his wife in causing the First World War?

    5

> The disarmament terms of the Treaty of Versailles upset many Germans.

2. Describe the military terms imposed on Germany by the Treaty of Versailles.

    4

SECTION B: ENQUIRY SKILLS

The following sources are about life in Britain and Germany during the First World War.

**Study the sources carefully and answer the questions which follow.
You should use your own knowledge where appropriate.**

Source A is a British government poster produced in 1914.

Source A

3. How useful is **Source A** as evidence of methods used by the British government to encourage men to enlist during the First World War?

    4

Page ten

Marks

In **Source B** an eyewitness remembers living in an English village in 1917.

Source B

> It was a terrible time, terrible. We were starving. I can remember my mother having to go out to pick dandelion leaves and then washing them and making sandwiches with them. We were forced to pick the greens off the turnips and cook them with potatoes, mashed up with margarine. We never saw a piece of meat for ages. Many days our mother would make a jug of custard for our dinner, and we ate it with bread and butter. I got sick of the sight of custard. I don't know how mother managed. I hated seeing her sitting at the table with an empty plate. "Mummy you're not eating?", I'd say. "I'm not hungry", she'd reply. Whatever she had was for my brother and myself. If it had gone on for many more months, I don't know what would have happened to us.

4. Discuss the attitude of the author of **Source B** towards food supply in Britain during the First World War.　　3

Source C is the view of a German politician in 1917.

Source C

> How long can it go on? The food situation is unbearable. The bread ration was reduced this spring and the potato supply has been insufficient. During the past month most labourers have had to live on dry bread and a little meat. Undernourishment is spreading. These conditions do not make for good health. When we honestly face up to this situation we just have to say "our strength is totally spent".

5. To what extent do **Sources B** and **C** agree that conditions for civilians were difficult during the First World War?　　5

[END OF CONTEXT IIB]

Marks

UNIT II—INTERNATIONAL COOPERATION AND CONFLICT

> ### CONTEXT C: 1930s–1960s

SECTION A: KNOWLEDGE AND UNDERSTANDING

> Hitler wanted the Sudetenland to become part of Germany.

1. How important was the Czech Crisis of 1938 as a cause of growing tension in Europe up to September 1939?

   5

> In 1945 the British Empire seemed as strong as ever but things had changed.

2. Describe Britain's decline as a world power between 1945 and 1960.

   4

SECTION B: ENQUIRY SKILLS

The following sources are about the problems faced by the people of Britain and Germany during the Second World War.

Study the sources carefully and answer the questions which follow. You should use your own knowledge where appropriate.

Source A is a British government poster from 1939.

Source A

3. How useful is **Source A** as evidence of how the British government protected civilians from air raids during the Second World War?

   4

Source B was written by a British woman after the Second World War.

Source B

> I was working at Wills Tobacco Company in Bristol when war broke out in September 1939. I didn't like the air-raid shelters because they made the noise of the bombs even louder. We often just stayed at home and slept under the table. Food was scarce but I was relieved that it never ran out, and a lot was done to distribute it fairly. Many things were rationed; sugar, tea, eggs and cheese for example. Yet other things like potatoes and carrots were quite plentiful so we ate a lot of them. I was reasonably happy that our diet was healthy but there was not a lot of variety. I didn't like the clothes coupons much. We had to collect coupons to buy a new dress or curtains or something like that.

4. Discuss the attitude of the author of **Source B** to food supplies in Britain during the Second World War.

3

Source C is from "Era of the Second World War" by Carole Brown.

Source C

> Life was not so easy after 1942 when many German cities were bombed. Some 400,000 Germans were killed in the bombing raids. The German people suffered food shortages and lots of items were rationed. Household goods and clothes were available only on a points system. However, price controls stopped inflation and food was shared out more fairly. As long as Germany remained a fighting force, full employment in essential industries made poorer families better off.

5. To what extent do **Sources B** and **C** agree about shortages in Britain and Germany during the Second World War?

5

[END OF CONTEXT IIC]

Marks

UNIT III—PEOPLE AND POWER

CONTEXT A: USA 1850–1880

SECTION A: KNOWLEDGE AND UNDERSTANDING

> Many white men distrusted and feared the Native Americans or despised them, like their Black American slaves, as an inferior race.

(Note: for this answer you should write a short essay of several paragraphs including an introduction and a conclusion.)

1. Explain why conflict developed in America as a result of white attitudes towards:

EITHER

(a) Black American slaves before 1860

8

OR

(b) Native Americans after 1865.

8

SECTION B: ENQUIRY SKILLS

The following sources are about the problems facing Black Americans during Reconstruction.

Study the sources carefully and answer the questions which follow.
You should use your own knowledge where appropriate.

Source A is from "America" by G. Tindall and D. Shi.

Source A

> The Black Codes were laws passed by Southern states after the Civil War. Although they gave freed slaves certain rights, these laws imposed such severe restrictions that many people thought slavery was on the way back. The details of the Black Codes varied from state to state but some provisions were the same like prohibiting the right of freedmen to vote. Freed slaves could testify in courts but only when their own race was involved. They were obliged to sign a Labour Contract every year with punishments if the contracts were broken.

2. How fully does **Source A** explain why the Black Codes made life difficult for freed slaves after 1865?

   You must use evidence **from the source** and **from your own knowledge** and give reasons for your answer.

5

Marks

Source B is from "The United States 1850–1880".

Source B

> After the Civil War, the new Southern governments passed laws which limited most opportunities for freed slaves. In some cases the Codes left freedmen not much better off than they had been before the 1863 Emancipation Declaration. They were kept from giving evidence against Whites in all court trials. On the work front, they had to sign annual binding agreements with their employers with strict penalties if the terms were breached. Many Northerners believed that the laws were in effect re-establishing slavery.

3. To what extent do **Sources A** and **B** agree about the problems facing Black Americans during Reconstruction?

4

[END OF CONTEXT IIIA]

Marks

UNIT III—PEOPLE AND POWER

CONTEXT B: INDIA 1917–1947

SECTION A: KNOWLEDGE AND UNDERSTANDING

The impact of the British Raj on all aspects of Indian life was far reaching.

(Note: for this answer you should write a short essay of several paragraphs including an introduction and a conclusion.)

1. Explain the effects on India of British control of:

EITHER

(a) the Indian economy   8

OR

(b) Indian government and society.   8

SECTION B: ENQUIRY SKILLS

The following sources relate to Direct Action, 1946–1947.

**Study the sources carefully and answer the questions which follow.
You should use your own knowledge where appropriate.**

Source A was written by a journalist called Nikhil Chakravartty.

Source A

> On that night of 15–16th August, when it all began, it was only the presence of mind of some Muslim journalists which saved my life when I came across the rioting. I had never seen such devastation. Although this was not a war there were hundreds of people lying dead on the roadside, and still the fires burned all over the place. Many shops were being looted and many houses were burned down. On the third day, I came back home where I found to my horror an old Muslim washerman being beaten up; civilised people who knew him were doing it.

2. How fully does **Source A** describe the events during the days of Direct Action?

   You must use evidence **from the source** and **from your own knowledge** and give reasons for your answer.   5

Marks

Source B was written by Stanley Taylor of the Indian Police.

Source B

> The scenes which took place on that night in August were indescribable. The British were no longer the target of the rioters. Armed with every conceivable kind of weapon, the rioters slaughtered the young and the old, men and women without restraint. The streets were piled high with corpses. Shops were looted, houses were burnt and thousands of people rendered homeless. Soon the bazaar areas were ablaze. A pall of smoke from burning houses hung over the city. It will never be known how many were killed.

3. To what extent do **Sources A** and **B** agree about the days of Direct Action? **4**

[END OF CONTEXT IIIB]

Marks

UNIT III—PEOPLE AND POWER

CONTEXT C: RUSSIA 1914–1941

SECTION A: KNOWLEDGE AND UNDERSTANDING

> The Communists tried several policies to improve the economy of the Soviet Union.

(Note: for this answer you should write a short essay of several paragraphs including an introduction and a conclusion.)

1. Explain the effects on Russia of:

EITHER

   (*a*) Lenin's New Economic Policy   **8**

OR

   (*b*) Stalin's Five Year Plans.   **8**

SECTION B: ENQUIRY SKILLS

The following sources are about the problems facing Tsar Nicholas between 1914 and 1916.

**Study the sources carefully and answer the questions which follow.
You should use your own knowledge where appropriate.**

Source A is from "People and Power: Russia" by David Armstrong.

Source A

> In 1914 the First World War was greeted with great enthusiasm in Russia. Discontent with the Tsar's rule seemed to have been forgotten. At first, things went well but the situation became much worse in the next two years. The Tsar decided to take personal command of his retreating army but this made no difference and the soldiers' anger grew. In the cities, discontent arose as food was scarce, prices rose and people found it hard to stay warm. The peasants were growing less food because so many of them had been conscripted into the army.

2. How fully does **Source A** describe the problems facing Tsar Nicholas by 1916?

   You must use evidence **from the source** and **from your own knowledge** and give reasons for your answer.   **5**

Source B is from "Russia in Revolution" by John Taylor.

Source B

> By 1916 Russia was not a contented country. With unrest growing in the army, the situation in Russia was rapidly becoming worse. The mobilisation of so many peasants resulted in farms lying derelict when food was in short supply. Shortages of food, clothing and fuel made the cost of living in the cities more than most people could manage. Yet the trams were still running, the theatres were open and horse racing continued. Nevertheless, trouble was brewing and it was to explode the next year.

3. To what extent do **Sources A** and **B** agree about the problems facing the Tsar by 1916? **4**

[END OF CONTEXT IIIC]

Marks

UNIT III—PEOPLE AND POWER

CONTEXT D: GERMANY 1918–1939

SECTION A: KNOWLEDGE AND UNDERSTANDING

> Hitler attempted to transform German society with policies directed at youth and the Jewish people.

(Note: for this answer you should write a short essay of several paragraphs including an introduction and a conclusion.)

1. Explain the effects of Nazi policies between 1933 and 1939 towards:

   EITHER

   (*a*) young people

   OR

   (*b*) Jewish people.

8

8

SECTION B: ENQUIRY SKILLS

The following sources are about the weaknesses of the Weimar Government.

**Study the sources carefully and answer the questions which follow.
You should use your own knowledge where appropriate.**

Source A is from "Germany, 1918–1945" by J.A. Cloake.

Source A

> Throughout its life the Weimar Republic had few real supporters. It was always associated with the Peace Treaty and its dishonour. It was further disgraced by the French occupation of the Ruhr. Economically, Weimar Germany was saddled with the war debt and reparations. The period of inflation in the early 1920s created insecurity and suffering amongst all classes and most blamed it on the Weimar Government. When the Wall Street Crash triggered the Great Depression, the measures taken by the Weimar Government to cope with the crisis further angered the majority of Germans. Many looked for alternative solutions.

2. How fully does **Source A** show why the Weimar Republic was so unpopular?

   You must use evidence **from the source** and **from your own knowledge** and give reasons for your answer.

5

Marks

Source B is from "Hitler and the Third Reich" by Richard Harvey.

Source B

> The Weimar Republic had a difficult start. By signing the Treaty of Versailles, the Republic, however unfairly, was forever associated with it. It had also been left with a huge national debt and compensation money to pay. As hyperinflation set in, anyone with savings or pensions lost their money and, more importantly, their faith in the Weimar Republic. The American Stock Market crash marked the beginning of the end as Germany was particularly badly hit by the economic crisis which followed. Unable to agree on measures to deal with the Depression, the government lost the support of the people. Many disgruntled Germans began to turn to other political parties.

3. To what extent do **Sources A** and **B** agree about the problems experienced by the Weimar Republic?

4

[END OF CONTEXT IIID]

[END OF QUESTION PAPER]

[BLANK PAGE]

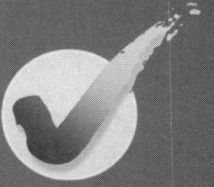

[BLANK PAGE]

G

1540/402

NATIONAL
QUALIFICATIONS
2007

FRIDAY, 18 MAY
10.20 AM – 11.50 AM

HISTORY
STANDARD GRADE
General Level

Answer questions from Unit I **and** Unit II **and** Unit III.

Choose only **one** Context from each Unit and answer Sections A **and** B. The Contexts chosen should be those you have studied.

The Contexts in each Unit are:

Use the information in the sources, and your own knowledge, to answer the questions.

Number the questions as shown in the question paper.

Some sources have been adapted or translated.

SCOTTISH
QUALIFICATIONS
AUTHORITY

©

Marks

UNIT I—CHANGING LIFE IN SCOTLAND AND BRITAIN

CONTEXT A: 1750s–1850s

SECTION A: KNOWLEDGE AND UNDERSTANDING

Study the information in the sources. You must also use your own knowledge in your answers.

Source A is from "The Courier" newspaper describing what happened at Peterloo in 1819.

Source A

> At St. Peter's Field in Manchester large crowds began to assemble. Each group, as they came through the streets, kept in military order, with banners and sticks shouldered. One banner was painted with the words "Die like men, and not be sold like slaves". It was twenty minutes to one o'clock before Henry Hunt appeared. He spoke to the crowd appealing for them to be peaceful.

1. Describe what happened at Peterloo in 1819.   **3**

Source B was written by William Cobbett in 1828 after he visited a cotton mill.

Source B

> In the cotton-spinning work, the child workers are kept in a heat of from eighty to eighty-four degrees. The workers are not allowed to send for water to drink, even in the heat of the factory. In addition, there is the dust which these unfortunate creatures have to inhale. The fact is that healthy men are made old and past work at forty years of age, and children can become deformed.

2. Why was working in a cotton mill harmful to children's health?   **4**

Marks

SECTION B: ENQUIRY SKILLS

The issue for investigating is:

> Conditions in Scotland's growing towns in the nineteenth century were bad for people's health.

Study the sources carefully and answer the questions which follow.
You should use your own knowledge where appropriate.

In **Source C** Doctor Laurie reports on a visit to a house in Greenock in 1842.

Source C

> I found the mother lying on straw on the floor, delirious from fever. The husband had died in the hospital from the same disease. Some of the children were out begging, and the two youngest were crawling on the wet floor. There was a puddle of sewage in the centre of the floor. The children were actually starving and the mother was dying.

3. How useful is **Source C** for investigating conditions in the growing towns of Scotland in the nineteenth century?

   3

Source D is from a report written by a Glasgow doctor after visiting the homes of cotton workers in 1833.

Source D

> The following is an example of the families visited. Andrew Bruce, a spinner, has a good room and kitchen on the third floor. There is a wash-house below. He pays a rent of £4 a year. Mrs Bruce has been six years married and is in excellent health. She has always been able to cook, wash, make and mend for her husband and her children. They have fresh meat three or four times a week and sometimes tea and coffee.

4. What evidence in **Source C** agrees with the view that conditions in the growing towns were bad for people's health?

   What evidence in **Source D** does **not** agree with the view that conditions in the growing towns were bad for people's health?

   5

5. How far do you agree that conditions in the growing towns in nineteenth century Scotland were bad for people's health?

   You must use evidence **from the sources** and **your own knowledge** to come to a conclusion.

   4

[END OF CONTEXT IA]

Now turn to the Context you have chosen in Unit II.

Marks

UNIT I—CHANGING LIFE IN SCOTLAND AND BRITAIN

CONTEXT B: 1830s–1930s

SECTION A: KNOWLEDGE AND UNDERSTANDING

Study the information in the sources. You must also use your own knowledge in your answers.

Source A is evidence given by an eleven year old child to the Children's Employment Commission in 1842.

Source A

> I open the air-doors for the putters from six in the morning till six at night. Mother wakes me up at five and gives me a piece of cake which is all I get till I return home. There is plenty of water in the pit. The pit I'm in, it's up to my knees. I did go to school before I was taken down the pit and I could read a bit then. I know I shall die young because many people do so in East Houses pits.

1. Why was working in a coal mine harmful to children's health?   4

Source B is from the "Aberdeen Journal" of November 30th, 1912.

Source B

> A sensation was created yesterday afternoon when three Suffragettes with "explosive bombs" were found in the Music Hall, three hours before Mr Lloyd George was to address a great meeting. The protestors were arrested. While Mr Lloyd George was departing in a motor car, a Suffragette threw a brick at the car. Then, just as he reached Glenburnie Park, another Suffragette, with a large stone in her hand, thrust it at the car and crashed it through the window.

2. Describe the militant tactics used by the Suffragettes.   3

Marks

SECTION B: ENQUIRY SKILLS

The issue for investigating is:

> Conditions in Scotland's growing towns in the nineteenth century were bad for people's health.

Study the sources carefully and answer the questions which follow.

You should use your own knowledge where appropriate.

Source C is from a lecture given in the early 1880s by J.B. Russell, Medical Officer of Health for Glasgow.

Source C

> At the present time, 25% of the population of Glasgow live in one-room houses. Those small houses cause Glasgow's high death rate, especially in childhood. One of every five born in a house of one room never sees the end of their first year. Of those who die so young, a third have never been seen in their sickness by a doctor. The bad air in the houses leads to death from lung disease at all ages. As a result of poor conditions, the streets are filled with bandy-legged children.

3. How useful is **Source C** for investigating conditions in the growing towns of Scotland in the nineteenth century?

3

Source D is from a report written by a Glasgow doctor after visiting the homes of cotton workers in 1833.

Source D

> The following is an example of the families visited. Andrew Bruce, a spinner, has a good room and kitchen on the third floor. There is a wash-house below. He pays a rent of £4 a year. Mrs Bruce has been six years married and is in excellent health. She has always been able to cook, wash, make and mend for her husband and her children. They have fresh meat three or four times a week and sometimes tea and coffee.

4. What evidence in **Source C** agrees with the view that conditions in the growing towns were bad for people's health?

   What evidence in **Source D** does **not** agree with the view that conditions in the growing towns were bad for people's health?

5

5. How far do you agree that conditions in the growing towns in nineteenth century Scotland were bad for people's health?

   You must use evidence **from the sources** and **your own knowledge** to come to a conclusion.

4

[END OF CONTEXT IB]

Now turn to the Context you have chosen in Unit II.

Marks

UNIT I—CHANGING LIFE IN SCOTLAND AND BRITAIN

CONTEXT C: 1880s–Present Day

SECTION A: KNOWLEDGE AND UNDERSTANDING

Study the information in the sources. You must also use your own knowledge in your answers.

Source A is from "Change in Scotland, 1880 – 1980".

Source A

Throughout the nineteenth century, working people in Scotland had a very hard life. In order to improve their working conditions, many skilled craft unions were formed in the 1880s. Later on, unskilled workers combined into larger trade unions. In 1889 dock workers marched through the streets carrying fish heads to show what they lived on. More people now believed that the poor should be able to join a trade union to fight for a better standard of living. Others hoped it would raise their wages.

1. Why did trade unions grow during the period 1880–1914?

4

Source B is from the "Aberdeen Journal" of November 30th, 1912.

Source B

A sensation was created yesterday afternoon when three Suffragettes with "explosive bombs" were found in the Music Hall, three hours before Mr Lloyd George was to address a great meeting. The protestors were arrested. While Mr Lloyd George was departing in a motor car, a Suffragette threw a brick at the car. Then, just as he reached Glenburnie Park, another Suffragette, with a large stone in her hand, thrust it at the car and crashed it through the window.

2. Describe the militant tactics used by the Suffragettes.

3

Marks

SECTION B: ENQUIRY SKILLS

The issue for investigating is:

> Conditions in Scotland's growing towns and cities from 1880 to 1939 were bad for people's health.

Study the sources carefully and answer the questions which follow.

You should use your own knowledge where appropriate.

Source C is from a lecture given in the early 1880s by J.B. Russell, Medical Officer of Health for Glasgow.

Source C

> At the present time, 25%, of the population of Glasgow live in one-room houses. Those small houses cause Glasgow's high death rate, especially in childhood. One of every five born in a house of one room never sees the end of their first year. Of those who die so young, a third have never been seen in their sickness by a doctor. The bad air in the houses leads to death from lung disease at all ages. As a result of poor conditions, the streets are filled with bandy-legged children.

3. How useful is **Source C** for investigating conditions in the growing towns and cities of Scotland in the period 1880–1939?

3

Source D is from "Expansion, Trade and Industry" by C. Culpin.

Source D

> By 1939, city life for working people had improved a little. Housing Acts forced Councils to demolish disease-ridden slums. Councillors recognised that health meant fresh air as well, so parks were provided in many towns and cities. Some lucky families were able to escape to a cleaner, healthier environment in the council housing estates which began to be built. However, there were never enough of these new houses.

4. What evidence in **Source C** agrees with the view that conditions in the growing towns and cities were bad for people's health?

    What evidence in **Source D** does **not** agree with the view that conditions in the growing towns and cities were bad for people's health?

5

5. How far do you agree that conditions in the growing towns and cities in Scotland from 1880 to 1939 were bad for people's health?

    You must use evidence **from the sources** and **your own knowledge** to come to a conclusion.

4

[END OF CONTEXT IC]

Now turn to the Context you have chosen in Unit II.

UNIT II—INTERNATIONAL COOPERATION AND CONFLICT

CONTEXT A: 1790s–1820s

SECTION A: KNOWLEDGE AND UNDERSTANDING

Study the information in the sources. You must also use your own knowledge in your answers.

Source A is from "The British Navy" by Oliver Warner.

Source A

> The men of the lower deck, who fired the guns and went aloft and won battles, had every reason for unrest. Many of them were tied to a life they loathed, enduring conditions which were dreadful. Their pay had not increased for nearly 150 years and deductions were made for the chaplain and for the surgeon who often had very little skill.

1. Explain why British sailors did not like life in Nelson's navy. 4

Source B comes from "A History of Modern Europe" by H.L. Peacock.

Source B

> By 1827, it was clear that the Great Powers could not remain permanently united on important European matters as had been hoped in 1815. The Congress System had really come to an end although the idea that the great states should attempt to settle affairs by agreement was by no means dead. Many important meetings were held and there was no major European war for forty years after the Congress of Vienna.

2. How important was the Congress System in maintaining peace in Europe after 1815? 3

SECTION B: ENQUIRY SKILLS

Marks

The following sources are about the effects of the Revolutionary Wars on civilians in Britain.

Study the sources carefully and answer the questions which follow.

You should use your own knowledge where appropriate.

Source C is a cartoon drawn in 1795. It shows the Prime Minister, William Pitt, as a butcher giving a customer some meat as bread is too expensive.

Source C

Price of food 1795

Mutton 10d per lb
Beef 10d per lb
Bread 12d a loaf

Wages per week 1795

Carpenter 12d
Shoemaker 10d
Farmer 7d

3. How useful is **Source C** as evidence of the effects of the Revolutionary Wars on people in Britain?

3

[Turn over

Marks

Source D describes the effects of the Revolutionary Wars upon British people.

Source D

> The Continental System interfered with trade and led to some unemployment but merchants often looked for new markets in South America. Farmers benefited from the drop in the amount of food being imported into Britain. This drop, however, led to increased prices for bread and other foodstuffs. For the workers this was a disaster as wages stayed low.

4. How far do **Sources C** and **D** agree about the effects of the Revolutionary Wars upon people in Britain?

4

Source E is part of a message from the French Government to the people of France.

Source E

> From this moment on, until our enemies have been driven out of the lands of the French Republic, all the French people are permanently enlisted into the service of the armies. Young men will go and fight. Married men will make arms and transport supplies. Women will make tents and clothes and serve in the hospitals. Children will make old linen into bandages. Old men will teach hatred of Kings.

5. How fully does **Source E** describe the effects of the Revolutionary Wars on the people in France?

You must use evidence **from the source** and **from your own knowledge** and give reasons for your answer.

4

[END OF CONTEXT IIA]

Now turn to the Context you have chosen in Unit III.

Marks

UNIT II—INTERNATIONAL COOPERATION AND CONFLICT

CONTEXT B: 1890s–1920s

SECTION A: KNOWLEDGE AND UNDERSTANDING

Study the information in the sources. You must also use your own knowledge in your answers.

Source A is taken from "Forgotten Voices of the Great War".

Source A

> By 1915, the trench system stretched for hundreds of miles. In a trench you can just imagine the agony of a fellow standing up to his waist in mud, with just his mess tin to bale the water out. Trench foot was common, owing to mud soaking through your boots. In many cases your toes nearly rotted off. When a fellow got a very high temperature, you could tell he'd probably got trench fever.

1. Explain why many soldiers were unhappy with life in the trenches.   **4**

Source B was written by historian John Clare.

Source B

> The League of Nations aimed to stop wars, encourage disarmament and enforce the Treaty of Versailles. Judged against these aims, the League was quite successful in the 1920s. It stopped border squabbles turning into wars. It solved a dispute between Sweden and Finland over the Aaland Islands in 1922. The League also improved people's lives.

2. How successful was the League of Nations in solving the world's problems in the 1920s?   **3**

[Turn over

Marks

SECTION B: ENQUIRY SKILLS

The following sources are about the Home Front in Britain during the First World War.

Study the sources carefully and answer the questions which follow.

You should use your own knowledge where appropriate.

Source C is a poster produced by the British Government in 1917.

Source C

3. How useful is **Source C** as evidence of women's contribution to the war effort during the First World War?

   3

Source D describes women's war work during the First World War.

Source D

> Many thousands of women became nurses. Some of these women had a chance to work abroad. Others worked in military hospitals and army bases in Britain. The Voluntary Aid Detachment was an organisation set up to provide help for the sick and wounded, in case of enemy invasion. For this work, the VADs were at first unpaid but, from 1915, they were paid £20 a year. Although they had free board and lodgings, they had to buy their uniform out of their earnings.

4. How far do **Sources C** and **D** agree about the work women did during the First World War?

   4

Source E is from "Britain and the Great War" by G. Hetherton.

Source E

> Desperate attempts were made to grow more food. Nearly everybody started to keep an allotment where they could grow food. The amount of land used for farming increased from eleven million acres in 1914 to fourteen million in 1918. However, many farmers had joined the army, and much of the work on the land was now carried out by the new Women's Land Army.

5. How fully does **Source E** describe the ways the British people managed to get food during the First World War?

   You must use evidence **from the source** and **from your own knowledge** and give reasons for your answer.   **4**

[*END OF CONTEXT IIB*]

Now turn to the Context you have chosen in Unit III.

Marks

UNIT II—INTERNATIONAL COOPERATION AND CONFLICT

CONTEXT C: 1930s–1960s

SECTION A: KNOWLEDGE AND UNDERSTANDING

Study the information in the sources. You must also use your own knowledge in your answers.

Source A is about Britain after the Second World War.

Source A

> The British people finally achieved victory in 1945. Britain came out of the Second World War poorer than in 1939. Fighting the war needed a lot of money. Britain had dug deep into the country's savings. A great deal of the nation's trade had been lost. The two new giants were the USSR and the USA. Britain was proud and victorious but was now no longer as great as it had been.

1. Explain why Britain was less powerful after 1945.   **4**

Source B describes the work of the United Nations Organisation.

Source B

> The UN Charter set out to save the world from the evil of war. Although the United Nations has not always succeeded in preventing conflicts, it has provided a place for discussions. It has sometimes dispatched a peacekeeping force. The achievement of the peacekeeping force in limiting minor wars has been very important. This was achieved in a divided Cyprus. Minor wars are not minor to the people caught up in them.

2. How successful was the United Nations in keeping the world peaceful after the Second World War?   **3**

Marks

SECTION B: ENQUIRY SKILLS

The following sources are about the Home Front in Britain during the Second World War.

Study the sources carefully and answer the questions which follow.
You should use your own knowledge where appropriate.

Source C is an official government poster used during the Second World War.

Source C

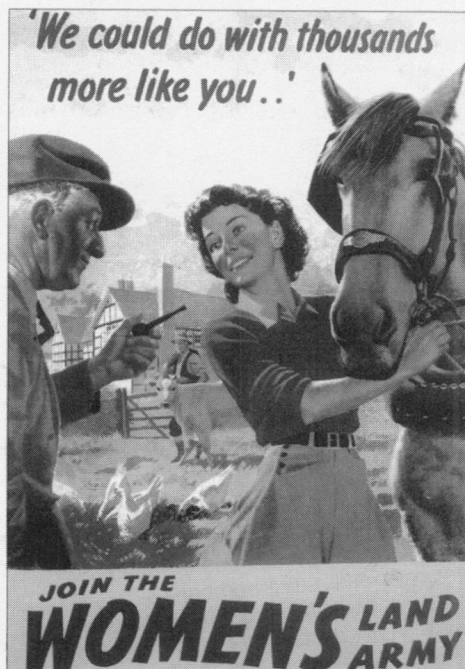

3. How useful is **Source C** as evidence of the role of British women during the Second World War?

3

In **Source D** a member of the Women's Land Army describes her work during the Second World War.

Source D

> I had lived in Leeds with my older sister. We both joined the Land Army at the same time and there were many hard days. I remember one bitterly cold day when we were told to lift parsnips. We had to try and kick the parsnips out of the frozen earth. A colleague appeared in an old, long coat which reached from her ears to her ankles. This was not what we had looked forward to when we volunteered.

4. How far do **Sources C** and **D** disagree about the working lives of women during the Second World War?

4

[Turn over

Marks

In **Source E** Kathleen Monham writes about her childhood during the Second World War.

Source E

> I was a school pupil during the Blitz. At night, people in towns had to be very careful not to show lights. This could let German bombers know where to drop their bombs. For the same reason, cars drove without lights. House windows had to be screened with dark material. Some people were very careless at first. I remember a very familiar sound from the warden: "Put out that light!"

5. How fully does **Source E** describe the effects of air raids during the Blitz?

   You must use evidence **from the source** and **from your own knowledge** and give reasons for your answer.   **4**

[END OF CONTEXT IIC]

Now turn to the Context you have chosen in Unit III.

Marks

UNIT III—PEOPLE AND POWER

CONTEXT A: USA 1850–1880

SECTION A: KNOWLEDGE AND UNDERSTANDING

Study the information in the sources. You must also use your own knowledge in your answers.

Source A is about slavery in the Southern states of America.

Source A

> By the 1850s, slaves made up about one third of the population in the South, although most farms and plantations employed less than 50 slaves. Some slave owners treated their slaves quite well. But many subjected their slaves to many rules and regulations. Discipline was harsh. Owners often broke up slave families. Slaves had little or no freedom to visit family or friends owned by other slave owners.

1. Explain why some people were opposed to slavery in America.   **3**

Source B is a description of the Confederate attack on Fort Sumter.

Source B

> The President took the view that after a state seceded, federal forts within the Confederacy became the property of the US government. On 12th April 1861, the Confederate commander, General Beauregard, demanded that Major Anderson surrender Fort Sumter in Charleston Harbour. Anderson replied that he would be willing to leave the fort when his supplies were exhausted. Beauregard rejected the offer.

2. Describe what happened at Fort Sumter in April 1861.   **3**

[Turn over

Marks

SECTION B: ENQUIRY SKILLS

The following sources are about life in the South during Reconstruction.

Study the sources carefully and answer the questions which follow.

You should use your own knowledge where appropriate.

In **Source C** Mrs Mary Platt remembers life in the South during the period of Reconstruction after the Civil War.

Source C

> Before the war we had good hogs but the war changed all that. Through the terrible days of Reconstruction, many people were unable to feed their livestock. There were no Negroes (African Americans) to work the farm and everything went to ruin. During the four years of war, times were hard enough but this only prepared the way for the suffering afterwards. The carpetbaggers stirred the freed slaves to lawlessness.

3. What was the attitude of Mrs Platt in **Source C** towards life in the South during Reconstruction?

3

Source D is from "America, A Narrative History".

Source D

> The defeat of the Confederacy changed much of Southern society. However, new Republican state governments in the South were very like the old ones. By introducing the Black Codes, they intended to preserve slavery as nearly as possible. These Codes gave African Americans certain new rights but also restricted their freedom. The homeless were punished with severe fines and could be sold into private service if unable to pay.

4. How fully does **Source D** describe how African Americans were treated in the South during the period of Reconstruction?

You must use evidence **from the source** and **from your own knowledge** and give reasons for your answer.

4

[END OF CONTEXT IIIA]

Marks

UNIT III—PEOPLE AND POWER

CONTEXT B: INDIA 1917–1947

SECTION A: KNOWLEDGE AND UNDERSTANDING

Study the information in the sources. You must also use your own knowledge in your answers.

Source A describes the importance of India to Britain.

Source A

> Britain had many colonies but India was by far the most important. To stress the importance of the colony, the Viceroy of India was paid twice as much as the British Prime Minister. India's huge population of around 300 million bought enormous amounts of British goods. India also supplied Britain with a wide range of cheap foods.

1. Explain why Britain wanted to keep control of India.   **3**

Source B is from "The British Raj" by Zachary Nunn.

Source B

> In some ways the Raj was a bluff. Some 300 million Indians were ruled by barely 1500 British administrators of the Indian Civil Service. There were about 3000 British Officers in charge of the Indian Army. Many British people thought this was as it should be. They thought that handing over power to the Indian people would bring disaster.

2. Describe in what ways the British controlled India.   **3**

[Turn over

Marks

SECTION B: ENQUIRY SKILLS

The following sources are about the partition of India and its effects upon Indians.

Study the sources carefully and answer the questions which follow.
You should use your own knowledge where appropriate.

In **Source C** Muhammad Ali Jinnah gives his views on the partition of India.

Source C

> I cannot imagine a united India, containing both Hindus and Muslims. Hindus and Muslims have different religions and social customs. To join two such nations together under a single state, one as a majority and the other as a minority, must lead to a growing discontent. This, in turn, would result in the final destruction of such a united state.

3. What was the attitude of Muhammad Ali Jinnah in **Source C** towards the future of India?

3

Source D describes the situation in India at the time of partition.

Source D

> The partition of India was not a simple matter and Gandhi was no longer able to influence developments. The partition of India led to millions of people becoming refugees. Muslims fled to Pakistan and Hindus flocked into India. Pakistan was torn into two parts, separated by one thousand miles of Indian territory.

4. How fully does **Source D** describe the problems caused by the partition of India?

You must use evidence **from the source** and **from your own knowledge** and give reasons for your answer.

4

[END OF CONTEXT IIIB]

Marks

UNIT III—PEOPLE AND POWER

CONTEXT C: RUSSIA 1914–1941

SECTION A: KNOWLEDGE AND UNDERSTANDING

Study the information in the sources. You must also use your own knowledge in your answers.

Source A describes Tsar Nicholas II.

Source A

> Nicholas II, Tsar of all the Russias, had been the Emperor for many years and was seen as an excellent family man. However, many Russians thought he was weak and too easily controlled by his German wife. They also thought he had too much power. In 1915 Nicholas took personal command of the Russian army but it continued to retreat.

1. Explain why many Russians disliked being ruled by the Tsar.   **3**

In **Source B** historian David Armstrong describes the Bolshevik Revolution of October 1917.

Source B

> The Provisional Government knew what the Bolsheviks were planning and had officer cadets and a women's battalion on duty at the Winter Palace. Red Guards took over most of the key points in Petrograd. By the morning of 25 October all railway stations, bridges and government offices were in Bolshevik hands. By the next morning the Winter Palace had been captured without much of a fight.

2. Describe how the Bolsheviks seized power in Petrograd in October 1917.   **3**

[Turn over

Marks

SECTION B: ENQUIRY SKILLS

The following sources are about Russia in the period of War Communism.

Study the sources carefully and answer the questions which follow.

You should use your own knowledge where appropriate.

Source C is from "The Russian Revolution" by John Quinn.

Source C

> By 1921, Russia had been at war for seven years, first against Germany and then against herself. Bad harvests produced one of the worst ever famines. Production dropped: steel making was down by 96% and coal mining down by 90%. The great cities were like ghost towns as workers fled to the countryside in search of food.

3. How fully does **Source C** describe the problems faced by the Russian people in 1921?

   You must use evidence **from the source** and **from your own knowledge** and give reasons for your answer.   **4**

Source D is from the Manifesto of the Kronstadt rebels, issued in 1921.

Source D

> We joined the Communist Party to help the workers and peasants. But under War Communism the worker has become the slave of the factory instead of its master. He cannot work where he wants to work or turn down work which is beyond his physical strength. Those who dare to say the truth are put in prison where they suffer torture or are shot.

4. What was the attitude of the authors of **Source D** towards War Communism?   **3**

[END OF CONTEXT IIIC]

UNIT III—PEOPLE AND POWER

CONTEXT D: GERMANY 1918–1939

SECTION A: KNOWLEDGE AND UNDERSTANDING

Study the information in the sources. You must also use your own knowledge in your answers.

Source A is from a German newspaper, published in 1919.

Source A

> The terms of the peace settlement conducted at Versailles have now been revealed. This treaty has left Germany a torn and tattered country. Germany has been denied the right to have any say in her own future. Large amounts of German territory have been torn off. This peace treaty is unacceptable.

1. Explain why many Germans hated the Treaty of Versailles.　　　　3

Source B is about the Spartacist Revolt of 1919.

Source B

> In January 1919 the Spartacists launched an armed uprising in Berlin. They aimed to seize power from Ebert, the leader of the new Provisional Government. Ebert could not rely on the army because it had been broken up after the Armistice was signed. Instead, he used the Freikorps: bands of ex-servicemen who hated socialism in any form. Brutally, the Freikorps crushed the Spartacist revolt.

2. Describe what happened during the Spartacist Revolt.　　　　3

[Turn over

Marks

SECTION B: ENQUIRY SKILLS

The following sources are about Church opposition to the Nazis.

Study the sources carefully and answer the questions which follow.

You should use your own knowledge where appropriate.

Source C is from "Germany 1918–1945" by Josh Brooman.

Source C

> Germany's Protestants belonged to twenty eight church groups. In 1933, under Nazi pressure, they agreed to unite to form a "Reich" Church. Many Protestants broke away and set up their own Confessional Church. This was a clear challenge to Nazi power. As a result, several hundred Confessional Church ministers were arrested and many were put into concentration camps. The Church's youth organisation was also banned.

3. How fully does **Source C** describe the steps taken by the Nazis to control the churches in Germany?

   You must use evidence **from the source** and **from your own knowledge** and give reasons for your answer.

   4

Source D is from a statement issued by the Confessional Church in Germany in 1935.

Source D

> The Nazis officially deny any intention to interfere in the life of the Confessional Church but in fact they constantly interfere. Several years ago the Nazis banned the Church's youth organisation. We are also alarmed that Christian influence in public life has grown weaker. In addition, the Confessional Church is ashamed that concentration camps still exist.

4. What is the attitude of the Confessional Church in **Source D** towards the Nazi Government?

   3

[END OF CONTEXT IIID]

[END OF QUESTION PAPER]

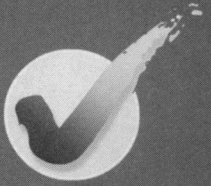

[BLANK PAGE]

C

1540/403

NATIONAL QUALIFICATIONS 2007

FRIDAY, 18 MAY 1.00 PM – 2.45 PM

HISTORY STANDARD GRADE Credit Level

Answer questions from Unit I **and** Unit II **and** Unit III.

Choose only **one** Context from each Unit and answer Sections A **and** B. The Contexts chosen should be those you have studied.

The Contexts in each Unit are:

Number the questions as shown in the question paper.

Some sources have been adapted or translated.

SCOTTISH QUALIFICATIONS AUTHORITY

©

Marks

UNIT I—CHANGING LIFE IN SCOTLAND AND BRITAIN

CONTEXT A: 1750s–1850s

SECTION A: KNOWLEDGE AND UNDERSTANDING

> The population began a dramatic increase, unprecedented in its continuity and size.

1.   Why did the population of Scotland increase between 1750 and 1820?   4

> Some farm houses in the late eighteenth century began to show signs of improvement.

2.   Describe housing conditions in the countryside in the late eighteenth century.   4

SECTION B: ENQUIRY SKILLS

The issue for investigating is:

> The Agricultural Revolution between 1750 and 1850 benefited everyone in Scotland.

**Study the sources carefully and answer the questions which follow.
You should use your own knowledge where appropriate.**

Source A was written by the Rev. Andrew Robertson, minister of Inverkeithing in Fife, in the New Statistical Account, 1845.

Source A

> Almost every piece of ground capable of cultivation is under the plough. Much waste land from moss has been reclaimed in the upper part of the parish. There is however no pasture except a small quantity on the steepest hills. There are no longer areas of common land. The lowest rent of land in the parish is £1 and 5 shillings (£1.25); the highest approaches £4. The average rent is nearer the higher figure. The leases are almost, without exception, for nineteen years.

3.   How useful is **Source A** for investigating the impact of the Agricultural Revolution in Scotland between 1750 and 1850?   4

Marks

Source B is by the historian T.C. Smout.

Source B

> Many features of the new farming did encourage emigration. The increase in the size of farms was said to lead to smaller populations. In many districts there had been great destruction of cottages and eviction of those people who were not essential to the day to day running of the farm. Small's plough alone halved the number of men needed to cultivate the land. On the other hand, the rise in wages for farm labourers showed that employers did not have it all their own way. The people remaining in the countryside were clearly somewhat better off in terms of their material standard of living.

Source C is from "The Case of Day-Labourers in Husbandry", written in 1795 by the Rev. D. Davies.

Source C

> The landowner, by uniting several small farms into one, is able to raise the rent considerably. Thus, thousands of farmers who formerly gained a livelihood on those separate farms have been gradually reduced to the class of day-labourers. But day-labourers sometimes cannot find work so they resort to the parish poor fund. It is a fact that thousands of parishes have now half the number of farmers which they had formerly. As the number of farming families has decreased, so the number of poor families has increased.

Look at Sources A, B and C.

4. What evidence is there in the sources that the Agricultural Revolution benefited people in Scotland?

   What evidence is there in the sources that the Agricultural Revolution did **not** benefit people in Scotland?

   6

5. How far do you agree that everyone in Scotland benefited from the Agricultural Revolution between 1750 and 1850?

   You must use evidence **from the sources** and **your own knowledge** to reach a **balanced conclusion**.

   5

[END OF CONTEXT IA]

Marks

UNIT I—CHANGING LIFE IN SCOTLAND AND BRITAIN

CONTEXT B: 1830s–1930s

SECTION A: KNOWLEDGE AND UNDERSTANDING

> The number of Scots continued to grow until the 1920s.

1. Why did the population of Scotland increase between 1830 and the 1920s?   **4**

> The houses which farm labourers lived in were often just as bad as those in the cities.

2. Describe housing conditions in the countryside in the late nineteenth century.   **4**

SECTION B: ENQUIRY SKILLS

The issue for investigating is:

> The coming of the railways brought benefits to all people in nineteenth century Scotland.

**Study the sources carefully and answer the questions which follow.
You should use your own knowledge where appropriate.**

Source A is from the written recollections of the railway engineer who was trying to build the Perth to Inverness Railway in the 1840s.

Source A

> I remember a visit to Cullen House to seek approval for the railway across the Seafield Estates on Speyside. Lady Seafield very decidedly told us that she hated railways. "Cheap travel", she said, "brought together such an objectionable variety of people." Lord Seafield was no more enthusiastic, maintaining that the railway would frighten away the grouse from his moors. "Besides", he went on, "what would become of the floaters—the men who have for many years been employed to float timber down the River Spey to the sea. Would a railway replace them?"

3. How useful is **Source A** for investigating attitudes to the building of railways in nineteenth century Scotland?   **4**

Marks

Source B is from "A Regional History of the Railways of Great Britain" by John Thomas and David Turnock.

Source B

> The effect of the railway on the North of Scotland is difficult to assess. With the reduction of transport costs, there was much greater competition to supply markets where previously there had been a near monopoly for local manufacturers. Consequently, prices went down. However, many workers found the railways were not so beneficial and their employment became less regular. With the influx of cheaper clothing, the manufacture of shawls and plaids in Kinross went into decline and all the local factories ceased to exist.

Source C is from "The Shaping of Nineteenth Century Aberdeenshire" by Sydney Wood.

Source C

> The flurry of activity that was an inevitable part of the construction of the railways alarmed the authorities. Navvies had earned a bad reputation and when they reached Inverness they found that the town had sworn in more special constables. The coming of the railways marked the decline of other transport methods. Coaching inns were replaced by new railway hotels which had modern facilities like hot showers. Inverurie lay, in the railway age, close to the heart of a complex network of rail routes and this proved a new stimulus to the industries in the town.

Look at Sources A, B and C.

4. What evidence is there in the sources that the coming of the railways benefited people in Scotland?

   What evidence is there in the sources that the coming of the railways did **not** benefit people in Scotland?   **6**

5. How far do you agree that the coming of the railways benefited all people in nineteenth century Scotland?

   You must use evidence **from the sources** and **your own knowledge** to reach a **balanced conclusion**.   **5**

[END OF CONTEXT IB]

UNIT I—CHANGING LIFE IN SCOTLAND AND BRITAIN

CONTEXT C: 1880s–Present Day

SECTION A: KNOWLEDGE AND UNDERSTANDING

> In the 60 years before the outbreak of World War Two, Scotland's population increased three-fold.

1. Why did the population of Scotland increase between 1880 and 1939?   **4**

> By the 1930s, rural housing conditions were still basic but better on the whole than in the industrial cities.

2. Describe housing conditions in the countryside in the first half of the twentieth century.   **4**

SECTION B: ENQUIRY SKILLS

The issue for investigating is:

> Technological change was the main reason that shipbuilding declined in Britain in the twentieth century.

Study the sources carefully and answer the questions which follow.
You should use your own knowledge where appropriate.

Source A is from the recollections of a retired British shipyard manager, written in the late 1980s.

Source A

> I've heard many opinions but, in my view, the collapse of the ship building industry in the 1960s was certainly the fault of the trade unions. Their attitude towards progress was really lamentable. The Swedes invented a small, portable hand-welding machine. In Sweden, four machines were worked by one man. The same happened in Germany and France. But in Britain, it was one man to one machine, so it took much longer for work to be done. The fact that the machine was automatic was what British shipyard workers objected to and the trade unions backed them up.

3. How useful is **Source A** for investigating the causes of the decline of British shipbuilding in the twentieth century?   **4**

Source B is from a history textbook written by historian Faith Geddes in 2002.

Source B

> After World War Two, the British government gave fewer subsidies than most foreign governments gave to their shipyards. Relations between management and men in British yards were often far from good. The frequent disputes and stoppages of work often led to late deliveries and setbacks to Britain's reputation as a shipbuilder. Only yards which adopted modern technology survived in Scotland. But even Yarrows, which pioneered glass-fibre hulls, were still forced to lay off men from time to time.

Source C describes problems with British shipbuilding in the twentieth century.

Source C

> A world slump in shipbuilding after World War Two affected Britain more than its rivals who modernised their yards and introduced the latest technology. On the other hand, British yards were slow to adapt to new technology. Industrial disputes over such factors as pay and conditions often resulted in strike action. Management attempts to introduce more modern, labour-saving devices led to lengthy demarcation disputes. Consequently, in 1985, Britain was producing only 2% of the world's new ships.

Look at Sources A, B and C.

4. What evidence is there in the sources that technological change was a reason for the decline in shipbuilding?

   What evidence is there in the sources to suggest that there were **other** reasons for the decline in shipbuilding?   **6**

5. How far do you agree that technological change was the main reason that shipbuilding declined in Britain in the twentieth century?

   You must use evidence **from the sources** and **your own knowledge** to reach a **balanced conclusion**.   **5**

[END OF CONTEXT IC]

Marks

UNIT II—INTERNATIONAL COOPERATION AND CONFLICT

CONTEXT A: 1790s–1820s

SECTION A: KNOWLEDGE AND UNDERSTANDING

> Everywhere the tide of sentiment turned against Napoleon.

(Note: for this answer you should write a short essay of several paragraphs including an introduction and a conclusion.)

1. In the Coalition victory over France by 1815, how important were:

EITHER

(*a*) the strengths of the Coalitions?   **8**

OR

(*b*) the weaknesses of the French?   **8**

SECTION B: ENQUIRY SKILLS

The following sources are about reaction to the events in France in the 1790s.

Study the sources carefully and answer the questions which follow. You should use your own knowledge where appropriate.

Source A is from "The Scottish Nation 1700–2000" by T.M. Devine.

Source A

> In December 1792, events in France took a dramatic turn. The bloodbath of the French nobility and clergy in the "September Massacres" attracted widespread coverage in the Scottish Press and it did not spare the readers any of the gory details of the grisly executions by guillotine. From this point on, the Revolution was represented as a grave threat to the entire social order. The French proceeded to terrify the ruling classes all over Europe in their Edict of Fraternity, offering military aid to all people seeking liberty from oppression.

2. How fully does **Source A** describe British reaction to events in France up to 1792?

You must use evidence **from the source** and **your own knowledge** and give reasons for your answer.   **5**

Marks

Source B is from a speech made by the British Prime Minister, William Pitt, in 1793.

Source B

> To insist upon the opening of the River Scheldt is an act which the French had no right to do. France has no right to cancel the laws regarding the Scheldt nor any other treaties between the Powers of Europe. England must act. If Holland had not applied to England when Antwerp was taken, the French would have overrun that territory. Unless we wish to stand by and suffer state after state coming under the power of the French, we must declare our firm resolution to oppose French ambition and aggrandisement which intend the destruction of England and of Europe.

3. Discuss the attitude of William Pitt in **Source B** towards France.   **3**

Source C is from "An Illustrated History of Modern Europe".

Source C

> After September 1792, the French set up a Republic and the French Revolutionary Army swept into the Austrian Netherlands. This established a French naval power on the Dutch coastline and threatened British control of the North Sea. The French also used Antwerp as a naval base, sending warships down the River Scheldt, ignoring Dutch neutrality and breaking the international Treaty of Utrecht. When all this was added to the French decrees of November, 1792, which promised to help all people wishing to recover their liberty from their own government, war between France and Britain became certain.

4. How far do **Sources B** and **C** agree about the French threat in 1792?   **5**

[*END OF CONTEXT IIA*]

Marks

UNIT II—INTERNATIONAL COOPERATION AND CONFLICT

CONTEXT B: 1890s–1920s

SECTION A: KNOWLEDGE AND UNDERSTANDING

The year was 1918 and the Great War was finally over.

(Note: for this answer you should write a short essay of several paragraphs including an introduction and a conclusion.)

1. In the Allied victory over Germany by 1918, how important was:

EITHER

(*a*) Allied use of new technology?   8

OR

(*b*) the collapse of the German home front?   8

SECTION B: ENQUIRY SKILLS

The following sources are about the causes of the First World War.

**Study the sources carefully and answer the questions which follow.
You should use your own knowledge where appropriate.**

Source A was said by Serbian nationalist, Dragutin Dimitrevic (called "Apis"), in 1912.

Source A

> War between Serbia and Austria is inevitable. If Serbia wants to live in honour, she can only do this by war. This war is determined by our duty to our traditions and our culture. This war results from the duty of our race which will not permit itself to be conquered by the Austrians. This war must bring about the everlasting freedom of Serbia, indeed of all the South Slavs in the Balkans. Our whole race must stand together to halt the attack of these aliens from Austria.

2. Discuss the attitude of Dragutin Dimitrevic in **Source A** towards Austria.   3

Marks

Source B is from "The Origins of the First World War" by James Joll.

Source B

> During the days immediately after the murder of the Archduke, the Austro-Hungarian government discussed what form of action it should take against Serbia. Serbia was disliked as it was accused of encouraging national feelings among the Southern Slavs inside the Austro-Hungarian Empire, and was therefore seen as a direct threat to the existence of the Empire. The assassination of Franz Ferdinand provided an excellent excuse for taking action against Serbia.

3. How far do **Sources A** and **B** agree about tension in the Balkans before World War One?

   5

Source C was written by historian Tony Allan.

Source C

> In 1879 Germany and Austria-Hungary signed a formal alliance and it was joined three years later by Italy creating the Triple Alliance. German foreign policy changed when Kaiser Wilhelm II came to power in 1888. Within months, Russia and France had entered negotiations with one another and, by 1893, they had formally allied. Germany was now faced with the prospect of someday having to fight a war on two fronts. Britain, feeling somewhat isolated, searched for allies and, in 1902, signed a treaty with Japan.

4. How fully does **Source C** describe the system of alliances and understandings in existence by 1914?

   You must use evidence **from the source** and **your own knowledge** and give reasons for your answer.

   5

[END OF CONTEXT IIB]

Marks

UNIT II—INTERNATIONAL COOPERATION AND CONFLICT

CONTEXT C: 1930s–1960s

SECTION A: KNOWLEDGE AND UNDERSTANDING

> The war in Europe ended with the surrender of Germany but continued in Asia and the Pacific until 2 September 1945.

(Note: for this answer you should write a short essay of several paragraphs including an introduction and a conclusion.)

1. In the Allied victory over Germany and Japan, how important was:

EITHER

(a) Allied use of new technology?   **8**

OR

(b) the efforts of civilians on the British home front?   **8**

SECTION B: ENQUIRY SKILLS

The following sources are about the causes of World War Two.

**Study the sources carefully and answer the questions which follow.
You should use your own knowledge where appropriate.**

Source A is part of a speech made by Hitler in 1934.

Source A

> We need space to make Germany independent. We must restore our great military strength. In the East, Germany must have mastery as far as the Caucasus Mountains. In the West, we will take the French coast. We need Belgium and Holland. Germany must become a colonial power equal to that of Britain. Germany must rule Europe or fall apart as a nation. In the centre, I shall place the steely core of a Greater Germany. Then we will take Austria and the Sudetenland. We will have a block of one hundred million people, without an alien element in it. If all this needs war, then so be it.

2. Discuss the attitude of Hitler in **Source A** towards Germany's place in Europe.   **3**

Marks

Source B is from "World War Two" by C. Bayne Jardine.

Source B

> In 1935 compulsory military service was brought back in Germany as it was in other countries. Germany was then able to agree an increase in its naval strength with Britain, and the Luftwaffe was being increased in strength. German industries now began to produce weapons of war. Hitler was prepared to risk a general war as he carried out his policies of territorial expansion. Hitler saw such a war as the price Germany had to pay for the pursuit of a German Empire.

3. How far do **Sources A** and **B** agree about Hitler's plans for Germany?   5

Source C is about the German attack on Poland.

Source C

> The next phase of Hitler's aggression was the plan to attack Poland, resulting in the start of aggressive war. Poland was attacked on September 1st, 1939. The German attack, code named Operation White (Fall Weiss), started at 04:45 hours when blitzkrieg tactics tore through the Polish forces. By the end of the month, Poland had surrendered to the Germans and the country was occupied.

4. How fully does **Source C** describe the attack on Poland in 1939?

   You must use evidence **from the source** and **your own knowledge** and give reasons for your answer.   5

[END OF CONTEXT IIC]

Marks

UNIT III—PEOPLE AND POWER

CONTEXT A: USA 1850–1880

SECTION A: KNOWLEDGE AND UNDERSTANDING

> Slavery was not the only source of tension between the North and the South.

1. How important was slavery as a cause of tension between the North and the South in 1860?   **4**

> The new Republican Party announced its main policies at a convention in Chicago on 16 May, 1860.

2. What were the main aims of the Republican Party in 1860?   **4**

SECTION B: ENQUIRY SKILLS

The following sources are about the Native American reaction to Westward expansion.

**Study the sources carefully and answer the questions which follow.
You should use your own knowledge where appropriate.**

Source A, titled "Emigrants Attacked by Comanches", was drawn for a book published in 1853 by Captain Seth Eastman, a soldier-artist who spent some time in frontier forts.

Source A

3. How useful is **Source A** as evidence of the ways in which the Native Americans reacted to Westward expansion?   **4**

Marks

Source B is part of an interview with Black Elk, a Sioux holy man.

Source B

> My people had lived in the Black Hills for many years. The white men wanted to have a road up through our country to the place where the yellow metal was. But my people did not want the road. It would scare the bison and make them go away. Also, it would let the other white men come in like a river. And so, when the white soldiers came and built themselves a fort, my people knew that they meant to have their road and take our country and maybe kill us all when they were strong enough.

4. How fully does **Source B** explain the reasons for the 1876 Sioux Revolt?

   You must use evidence **from the source** and **your own knowledge** and give reasons for your answer.

   4

[END OF CONTEXT IIIA]

Marks

UNIT III—PEOPLE AND POWER

CONTEXT B: INDIA 1917–1947

SECTION A: KNOWLEDGE AND UNDERSTANDING

> The British became increasingly unpopular in India in the twentieth century.

1. How important were economic factors in causing discontent with British rule by the 1930s?   **4**

> The Congress Party wanted to change the way India was ruled.

2. What were the main aims of the Congress Party?   **4**

SECTION B: ENQUIRY SKILLS

The following sources are about the reaction of Indians to British policies.

**Study the sources carefully and answer the questions which follow.
You should use your own knowledge where appropriate.**

Source A is a photograph showing followers of Gandhi making salt illegally on the beach at Dandi. It appeared in the "Bombay Chronicle" in April 1930.

Source A

3. How useful is **Source A** as evidence of Indian reaction to the Salt Tax?   **4**

Marks

Source B is from "The Far East and India" by P. J. Larkin.

Source B

> As the Second World War progressed, Britain faced problems in many areas. India was a major area of concern. In 1942 the British government sent Sir Stafford Cripps to India to try to get some agreement with Gandhi but the Indian leader demanded a full and immediate transfer of power to India. With the Japanese threatening Burma and Assam, the British had to refuse. Further terrorism and open revolt followed, and Gandhi was sent back to prison.

4. How fully does **Source B** describe the results of the Cripps Mission of 1942?

   You must use evidence **from the source** and **your own knowledge** and give reasons for your answer.

   4

[END OF CONTEXT IIIB]

Marks

UNIT III—PEOPLE AND POWER

CONTEXT C: RUSSIA 1914–1941

SECTION A: KNOWLEDGE AND UNDERSTANDING

> By the autumn of 1917 many Russians were losing patience with the Provisional Government.

1. How important was the First World War in causing discontent with the Provisional Government?

4

> The Bolsheviks wanted sudden and drastic changes in Russia.

2. What were the main aims of the Bolsheviks when they came to power in 1917?

4

SECTION B: ENQUIRY SKILLS

The following sources are about Stalin's policies in the 1930s.

**Study the sources carefully and answer the questions which follow.
You should use your own knowledge where appropriate.**

Source A is a Soviet government photograph from the 1930s. The words on the banner are "We demand collectivisation and the wiping out of the Kulaks".

Source A

3. How useful is **Source A** as evidence of how Russian peasants felt about Stalin's policy of collectivisation?

4

Marks

Source B is from "Russia and the USSR, 1905–1956" by Nigel Kelly.

Source B

> The Purges dominated politics in the USSR in the 1930s. Even now, historians argue over the causes. Stalin held show trials in which leading Communists confessed to trying to overthrow the government. Few, if any, of these people were guilty of the crimes to which they confessed. Their confessions often followed months of torture or a false promise that they would not be executed if they confessed. Thousands of other party members were sent to labour camps.

4. How fully does **Source B** describe Stalin's Purges?

   You must use evidence **from the source** and **your own knowledge** and give reasons for your answer.   **4**

[END OF CONTEXT IIIC]

UNIT III—PEOPLE AND POWER

CONTEXT D: GERMANY 1918–1939

SECTION A: KNOWLEDGE AND UNDERSTANDING

> As far as most Germans were concerned, the cause of their problems was the Weimar Republic.

1. How important were economic problems in making the Weimar Government unpopular by 1923?

4

> By 1933 there was a spectacular increase in the number of Germans who were willing to vote for the Nazis.

2. In what ways did the Nazi party manage to attract many German people by January 1933?

4

SECTION B: ENQUIRY SKILLS

The following sources are about the Nazis in power.

**Study the sources carefully and answer the questions which follow.
You should use your own knowledge where appropriate.**

Source A is a photograph of Nazis enforcing the boycott of Jewish-owned shops in 1933. The poster says "Germans fight back. Buy nothing Jewish."

Source A

3. How useful is **Source A** as evidence of the way the Nazis treated Jewish people?

4

Source B is from "Hitler's Germany" by Josh Brooman.

Source B

> In many ways life in Nazi Germany became more like military life. Many mass rallies took place. The most famous of them were held each year at Nuremberg in one of four specially built arenas outside the town. Just one of these arenas could hold 400,000 people. There they watched military parades and listened to choirs and to speeches. Each event at the rally was staged to perfection. At the 1937 rally, 100,000 men, each exactly 0.75 metres apart, marched past Hitler carrying 32,000 flags and banners.

4. How fully does **Source B** describe the military features of life in Nazi Germany?   **4**

    You must use evidence **from the source** and **your own knowledge** and give reasons for your answer.

[END OF CONTEXT IIID]

[END OF QUESTION PAPER]

Acknowledgements

Leckie & Leckie is grateful to the copyright holders, as credited, for permission to use their material:

Wendy Doran & Richard Dargie for extracts reproduced from *Change in Scotland 1830–1930* (2005 General p 6 and 2007 General p 6);

Philip Sauvain for an extract from *British Economic and Social History* (2004 General p 5 and 2006 Credit p 7);

Helena Shovelton for an extract from *An Illustrated History of Modern Britain*, 1783-1964 by D. Richards and J.W. Hunt (2004 General p 8);

Pulse Publications for an extract from *Appeasement and the Road to War* by R Cameron (2005 Credit p 10);

Getty Images for two photographs (2005 Credit p 13 and p 15);

Pulse Publications for extracts from *Changing Life in Scotland and Britain* by Cameron, Henderson and Robertson (2005 General pp 4, 5 and 2005 Credit pp 5, 10);

The National Maritime Museum for an extract from their website: www.nmm.ac.uk (2005 General p 8);

John Ray for an extract from *History for You – The Twentieth Century World* by J. Ray & J. Hagerty (2005 General p 12);

Adapted extracts from *Causes & Consequences of the African American Civil Rights Movement* by Michael Weber. Published by Evans Brother Ltd, 2A Portsman Mansions, Chiltern Street, London W1M 1LE. Copyright Evans Brothers Ltd © 1997. All rights reserved. (2005 General pp 14 & 15);

Solo Syndication for an illustration from *The London Evening Standard* (2005 General p 17);

The David King Collection for a poster (2005 General p 19);

Mary Evans Picture Library for a poster (2005 General p 21);

The Mirror Group for an extract from 'The new country life' by Richard Fenton, taken from *The Sunday Mail History of Scotland* (2006 General p 4);

Express Newspapers for an article taken from the *Daily Express*, 1909 (2006 General p 5);

The illustration 'And now let's learn to live together' from *The Daily Mirror* © Mirrorpix (2006 General p 16);

Extract from *Black People of America* by B. Rees & M .Sherwood. Reprinted by permission of Harcourt Education (2006 General p 19);

Anova Books for an extract from Nehru's autobiography in 1941 (2006 General p 20);

Extract from *Germany 1918–1939* by John Kerr. Reprinted by permission of Harcourt Education (2006 General p 24);

Extract from *America: A Native History* 4th edition by George Brown Tindall & David E Shi. Copyright © 1996, 1992, 1988, 1984 by W.W. Norton & Company Inc. Used by permission of W.W. Norton & Company, Inc (2006 Credit p 14 and 2007 General p 18);

Scott Ferris Associates for an extract from *The Last Days of the Raj* by T Royle (2006 Credit pp 16 & 17);

Getty Images for the cartoon *The British Butcher* (2007 General p 9).

The following companies/individuals have very generously given permission to reproduce their copyright material free of charge:

Hodder and Stoughton for extracts from *Scotland and Britain, 1830-1980* by Chalmers and Cheyne (2006 General p 5);

Extracts from *The Oxford Companion to Scottish History* by Lynch, Michael (2001). By permission of Oxford University Press (2005 General p 2 and 2006 General p 2);

Hodder & Stoughton for an extract from *Success in British History* by Peter Lane (2005 General p 8);

Random House for an extract from *The First World War* by John Keegan (2005 General p 10);

HMSO for an extract from *Landships, British Tanks in the First World War* by David Fletcher. © Crown copyright (2005 General p 10);

Pearson Education for an extract from *Hitler's Germany 1933-1945* by Josh Brooman (2005 General p 12);

Pearson Education for extracts from *The Penguin History of the United States* by Hugh Brogan (2005 General p 14 and 2006 General p 19);

Learning & Teaching Scotland for an extract from *The House Divided – America 1850–1865* (2005 General p 15);

Extract from *Divide & Quit* by Sir Penderal Moon. Reproduced by permission of the Executors of the estate of Sir Penderal Moon (2005 General p 17);

Cambridge University Press for an extract from *Russia & the USSR* by Philip Ingram, published in 1997

(2005 General p 18);

Pearson Education for an extract from *Russia in War & Revolution* by Josh Brooman (2005 General p 18);

Hodder & Stoughton for an extract from *Russia & The USSR 1900–1995* by Terry Fiehn (2005 General p 19);

Extract from *Forgotten Voices of the Great War* by Max Arthur, published by Ebury Press. Reprinted by permission of The Random House Group Ltd. (2005 General p 20);

Hodder & Stoughton for an extract from *People & Power: Germany* by I. Matheson (2005 General p 20);

Pearson Education for an extract from *Hitler & Germany* by B.J. Elliot (2005 General p 21);

Pearson Education for an extract from *Weimar Germany, 1918–1933* by Josh Brooman (2005 General p 21);

Extract from *Scotland: A New History* by Michael Lynch. Reprinted by permission of The Random House Group Ltd. (2005 Credit p 3);

John Donald Publishers (Birlinn) Ltd for an extract from *Modern Scottish History* by A. Cooke and I. Donnachie (2005 Credit p 3);

Hodder & Stoughton for an extract from *Years of Change* by J. Patrick & M. Packham (2005 Credit p 5);

Extract from *A Century in Photographs – Travel* by Ian Harrison. Reprinted by permission of HarperCollins Publishers Ltd © Ian Harrison 2000 (2005 Credit p 7);

Pearson Education for an extract from *A Social and Economic History of Industrial Britain* by Robottom (2005 Credit p 7);

Peter Vansittart for an extract from *Voices* 1870–1914 (2005 Credit p 9);

Express Newspapers for an extract from a speech by David Lloyd George (2005 Credit p 9);

Extract from *The American West, 1840-95* by T. Boddington. Reprinted by permission of HarperCollins Publishers Ltd © James Green 1977 (2005 Credit p 12);

Cambridge University Press for an extract from *The American West* by Mike Mellor (2005 Credit p 13);

Extract from *The Rise and Fall of the Great Powers* by Paul Kennedy. Reprinted by permission of HarperCollins Publishers Ltd © Paul Kennedy 1988. (2005 Credit p 16);

The University of Exeter Press for an extract from *Nazism 1919–1945 Volume Two: State, Economy & Society* 1933-1939 edited by J Noakes & G Pridham, new edition 2000. (2005 Credit p 19);

Photograph courtesy of the Imperial War Museum, London (2005 Credit p 19);

The Penguin Group for two extracts adapted from *The Scottish Nation 1700-2000* by T. M. Devine (2005 General p 3 and 2006 General p 4);

Adam & Charles Black for an extract from *Memorials of His Time* by Henry Cockburn (2006 General p 3);

HarperCollins Publishers for an extract from *A History of the Scottish People* by T. C. Smout (2006 General p 3);

Pearson Education for an extract from *Changing Lives* by Sydney Wood (2006 General p 6);

Hodder & Stoughton for an extract from *British Social and Economic History* by Ben Walsh (2006 General p 6);

Extract from *Trafalgar, the Nelson Touch* by David Howarth, published by Weidenfeld and Nicolson, a division of the Orion Publishing Group (2006 General p 8);

Pearson Education for an illustration from *An Illustrated History of Modern Europe* 1789-1945 (2006 General p 9);

Extract adapted from David Evans, *Teach Yourself First World War* (Hodder Arnold, 2004), (c) 2004 David Evans, reproduced by permission of Hodder & Stoughton (2006 General p 11);

HarperCollins Publishers for an extract from *Making History, World History from 1914 to the Present Day* by C. Culpin (2006 General p 11)

Cambridge University Press for an extract from *Modern World History* by T McAleavy, P Grey, R Little (2006 General p 13);

Chambers Harrap Publishers Ltd for an extract from *Conflict and Cooperation 1930–1960* by Richard Dargie & Wendy Doran (2006 General p 15);

Two extracts from *Our World Today* (Oxford University Press 1985) by permission of the publisher (2006 General p 17);

Pearson Education for an extract from *The American West* 1840-95 by Rosemary Rees (2006 General p 18);

The Penguin Group for an extract adapted from *Empire 2003* by Professor Niall Ferguson (2006 General p 20);

Hodder & Stoughton for an extract from *Reaction and Revolution* by Michael Lynch (2006 General p 22);

Cambridge University Press for an extract from *Germany 1918–1945* by P. Grey & R. Little (2006 General p 24);

Pearson Education for an extract from *Germany 1918–1945* by J. Brooman (2006 General p 25);

Hodder & Stoughton for an extract from *Germany 1918–1945* by Greg Lacey & Keith Shepherd (2006 General p 25);

Scottish Record Office for an extract from *Report to Highland Destitution Commission* HD61 and *The Scots in Canada* (2006 Credit p 3) © Crown copyright (2006 Credit p 2 and p 3);

Birlinn Ltd for an extract from *Lowland Perceptions of the Highlands and the Clearances during the famine years 1845-1855* by Krisztina Fenyo (2006 Credit p 4);

Strathclyde Regional Council Archives for an extract from *Support Pack on Changing Life* (2006 Credit p 5);

Pearson Education for a cartoon from *Modern Europe* by D. Richards (2006 Credit p 8);

The Imperial War Museum for two posters (2006 Credit pp 10 & 12);

Hodder & Stoughton for an extract from *Cooperation & Conflict 1890–1930* by J. Harkness, H. McMillan & D. Moore (2006 Credit p 11);

Folens Publishers for an extract from *Era of the Second World War* by Carole Browne (2006 Credit p 13);

Hodder & Stoughton for an extract from *People & Power: Russia* by David Armstrong (2006 Credit p 18);

HarperCollins Publishers for an extract from *Russia in Revolution* by John L Taylor (2006 Credit p 19);

Oxford University Press for an extract from *Germany 1918-45* by John Cloake (2006 Credit p 20);

Nelson Thornes for an extract from *Hitler & the Third Reich* by R Harvey (2006 Credit p 21).

Aberdeen Journals for two extracts from *The Aberdeen Journal*, 1912 (2007 General p 6);

DC Thomson & Co for an article from *The Courier* (2007 General p 2);

HarperCollins Publishers for an extract from *Expansion, Trade and Industry* by C Culpin (2006 Credit p 7 and 2007 General p 2);

Random House for an extract from *Forgotten Voices of the Great War* by Max Arthur (2007 General p 11);

Pearson Education for an extract from *The World Re-made: The Results of the First World War* by Josh Boorman (2007 General p 2);

Imperial War Museum for a poster produced by the British Government in 1917 (2007 General p 12);

Random House for two extracts from *How We Lived Then* by Longmate (2007 General p 12 and 2007 General p 15);

Pearson Education for an extract from *Germany 1918-45* by Josh Brooman (2007 General p 23);

The Penguin Group for an extract from *The Scottish Nation 1700-2000* by T M Devine (2007 Credit p 8);

Pearson Education for an extract from *An Illustrated History of Modern Europe* by Richards and Hunt (2007 Credit p 9);

Pearson Education for two extracts from *The Origins of the First World War* by James Joll (2007 Credit pp 10-11);

www.historylearningsite.co.uk for an extract (2007 Credit p 13);

Nicollet County Historical Society for the painting *Emigrants Attacked by Comanches* by Captain Seth Eastman (2007 Credit paper p 14);

Pearson Education for an extract from *Hitler's Germany* by Josh Brooman (2007 Credit p 21).